PRINCIPLES OF INVESTIGATIVE DOCUMENTATION

ABOUT THE AUTHORS

Philip Becnel has been an investigator in the private sector since 1999. He also wrote *Private Investigator Entry Level (02E)*, the only textbook for the entry course required for all private investigators in the Commonwealth of Virginia. He has a Bachelor of Arts in Anthropology from George Mason University and a Master of Criminal Justice degree from Boston University. Philip is presently the managing partner of Dinolt, Becnel & Wells Investigative Group in Washington, DC, where he lives with his wife and two children.

Scott J. Krischke has conducted investigations as a journalist, law clerk and investigator since 2005. He has been published in several domestic and international news publications and in the *Journal of Law and Policy*. He holds a Bachelor of Arts in Communications-Journalism from DePaul University and a Juris Doctorate from Brooklyn Law School. A native of Chicago, Mr. Krischke presently resides in New York City.

PRINCIPLES OF INVESTIGATIVE DOCUMENTATION

Creating a Uniform Style for Generating
Reports and Packaging Information

By

PHILIP A. BECNEL IV

and

SCOTT J. KRISCHKE

CHARLES C THOMAS • PUBLISHER, LTD.
Springfield • Illinois • U.S.A.

Published and Distributed Throughout the World by

CHARLES C THOMAS • PUBLISHER, LTD.
2600 South First Street
Springfield, Illinois 62704

This book is protected by copyright. No part of
it may be reproduced in any manner without
written permission from the publisher.
All rights reserved.

©2012 by CHARLES C THOMAS • PUBLISHER, LTD.

ISBN 978-0-398-08697-8 (paper)
ISBN 978-0-398-08698-5 (eBook)

Library of Congress Catalog Card Number: 2011029243

With THOMAS BOOKS *careful attention is given to all details of manufacturing and design. It is the Publisher's desire to present books that are satisfactory as to their physical qualities and artistic possibilities and appropriate for their particular use.* THOMAS BOOKS *will be true to those laws of quality that assure a good name and good will.*

Printed in the United States of America
CR-R-3

Library of Congress Cataloging-in-Publication Data

Becnel, Philip.
 Principles of investigative documentation : creating a uniform style for generating reports and packaging information / by Philip Becnel and Scott James Krischke.
   p. cm.
 Includes index.
 ISBN 978-0-398-08697-8 (pbk.) -- ISBN 978-0-398-08698-5 (ebook)
 1. Criminal investigation. 2.Documentation. I. Krischke, Scott James. II. Title.

HV8073.B375 2012
651.5'042--dc23
                                            2011029243

This book is dedicated to Philip V and Ava, and to future investigators everywhere.

INTRODUCTION

I am a firm believer that investigative documentation is the key to conducting a successful investigation, especially in the private sector. Investigative work is only as good as the way it can be communicated to a client, and the significant skills necessary to conduct an interview, a background investigation or surveillance are insufficient alone to conduct an investigation. Without proper documentation, the evidence gleaned during a good interview is not actionable and is t herefore largely useless. An investigator must get into the habit of viewing every action undertaken during an investigation–every database inquiry, every question, every response, every observation–as something that he or she may have to testify about at a later date. To buttress this possible testimony, he or she simply must adhere to the *Principles of Investigative Documentation*. Although I may have coined the title of this book, I did not invent these principles; they are the result of the evolution of private investigations over time. Although most of the work of investigators takes place outside of courtrooms, our effectiveness tends to live or die the first time we take the stand. Because clients and courts do not allow investigators to hit a restart button when it comes to documentation, once a report or a statement has been prepared and shared with the client, it is very difficult to take it back. The documents we prepare instantly become inextricably bound with the evidence that they purport to describe.

Moreover, documentation is particularly important in the private sector, because private investigation is fundamentally the business of selling the information we uncover and put into our investigative reports to clients for a fee. At the end of the investigation, it is not only what a witness told you that matters, but also how well you were able to document what they told you. Simply put: style, format, grammar and syntax matter. The biggest component of investigative documentation is superior communication, which is why this book is primarily about how to communicate more effectively. Teaching how to effectively communicate, however, is not an easy task, as investigators—like most adults—are often set in their ways. This may be especially true of investigators who learned how to document their investigations while working in law enforcement, where the pressure to produce flawless reports is decidedly less than it is in the private sector. A police officer will still have a job, even if he or she habitually mixes up past and present participles, but a private investigator who does not have a firm grasp of the English language will not be a private investigator for very long. In any case, bad habits die hard, and ultimately, one cannot teach a poor communicator how to be a superior communicator any easier than one could teach a lifelong extrovert how to become an introvert.

Still, I do believe that it is possible to teach even an investigator who happens to be a poor communicator how to appear, at least, like an *adequate* communicator in the way that he or she documents an investigation. This can be done by creating a clear standard, a uniform style and a common guidebook for generating reports and packaging information. A part of this standard is requiring that all investigative reports be subject to editorial review prior to being sent to a client. Another component is employing templates and reference tools to ensure that every report and every statement is consistent in style and meets the same high standards. However, the most important process in improving the quality of our documentation as investigators is forming daily habits built upon a foundation of sound business practices. Good communication begins with better note-taking in the field and with greater self-reflection when we step back from the subjects of our investigations. In this book, we will advocate strongly for taking notes about everything and for keeping a running resume, which essentially is a chronological journal regarding everything that happens in a case. Note-taking ensures accuracy. Making running resumes a daily part of our investigative routine ensures that nothing is ever missed. Our guidelines and the editorial review process ensure that our reports are uniformly consistent and free of substantive and grammatical errors. Clients can trust that the content of our reports and statements are accurate because their style, format, syntax, grammar and punctuation are meticulous. They can trust the quality of our investigations because, when we are called to testify, our documentation covers all conceivable angles of the case. In other words, sometimes presentation and habit can be just as important as substance.

This book was originally intended to guide the documentation practices for the investigators at my firm, Dinolt Becnel & Wells Investigative Group. It is the culmination of nearly 12 years of experience fretting over the best way to document investigations. Again, we did not invent these principles—but that does not mean that they are easy to find codified elsewhere in the hundreds of books that have been written over the years about how to investigate. While it is true that law enforcement agencies train their officers on how to employ their agencies' unique styles and formats, these policies tend not to transfer well into the private sector, because the purpose and many of the rules of law enforcement investigations are not the same as for private investigations. In any case, I never had the benefit of law enforcement experience, and nobody ever took me aside at the beginning of my career and showed me the best way to take notes, how to keep a running resume, how to write reports or how to take a statement from a witness. I learned these things largely by watching how other investigators documented their cases—and I also learned about the perils of sloppy documentation practices the hard way, by having to testify in my cases and explain the outcome of my investigations in minute detail under the terse questioning of opposing counsel.

I recall once having to testify to impeach the key government witness in a murder case where I failed to put a period or any other type of delineation between the following phrases, which were written on three separate lines in my notes: "may have been shooter," "unsure" and "read entire statement." In an earlier statement, the witness had sworn under oath that the defendant was not the shooter. The prosecutor, who was afforded a copy of my notes, seized on the ambiguity of whether the word "unsure" referred to whether the witness was unsure the defendant was the shooter (which is what I meant to write and what the witness actually said), or whether it referred to whether *I* was unsure that the witness read the entire statement he had provided earlier to another investigator. I was grilled at length on the issue, which was essentially the crux of the case, all because I failed to use a period after the first line. Thankfully, the defendant was acquitted regardless, so my sloppy note-taking did not have the consequence of sending an innocent person to prison—but after that experience I always pay attention to every detail, including punctuation marks.

Anyway, as my firm grew and we began hiring investigators, I passed my knowledge of documentation along to my associates, and this too was often a matter of trial and error. I quickly learned that great investigators are not always great writers. I had to figure out ways to make sure that the reports my investigators produced, for example, met the same high standards that I had for my own reports. I also needed to help my investigators avoid some of the mistakes that I had made.

The seed of this book was planted as a short style guide prepared by one of my staff investigators, Scott Krischke, who eventually left for New York to become a lawyer but remained with our firm as a contract editor while still in law school. Scott's style guide included things like when to capitalize titles and how to properly write numbers in reports. Before joining our firm he had been a journalist, so much of the information in these guidelines came from the Associated Press style to which he was accustomed. When it came time to write this book, it seemed only natural to invite Scott to be my co-author and to add some of the things that he learned about documentation in law school.

Much of Scott's original style guide is contained in the appendix of this book, although our firm's style has evolved over the years to make it more applicable for investigators, as opposed to journalists. The rationale for how and why we made these changes has largely been lost over the years, so readers will have to trust that my business partners and I have spent an inordinate amount of time at various stages of our partnership debating, for example, whether "also known as" should be written as "AKA" or "a/k/a," or whether it is more fitting to refer to someone as "black" or "African American" in an investigative report. Some of our decisions on these and other issues have surely boiled down to aesthetics or how other investigative entities have opted to dictate their style, but more often we made these types of decisions based upon a desire to avoid confusion and to maintain consistency and professionalism in our reports. This is not to claim that ours is necessarily the best way of doing things—but I do feel strongly that our style guidelines are the best way of doing things at *our* firm—and that other private investigative firms could undoubtedly stand to learn a lot by the great importance that we have placed on making our documentation practices perfect.

Most of the chapters in this book were the result of finally writing down everything that I have come to expect from my investigators regarding note-taking, keeping running resumes, writing reports and document retention. I included what basically amounts to an exhaustive section in the appendix on using abbreviations in notes, because I see the failure to memorize and use abbreviations in the field as a noteworthy (no pun intended) deficiency for many of the investigators I have trained and supervised over the years. I also conducted further research on investigative documentation in general before I chose to write this book. For example, I thoroughly reviewed the documentation guidelines used by the FBI to look for ways that our firm's guidelines could be improved, and I solicited feedback from several seasoned colleagues to gather their input about these topics.

Scott wrote Chapter 3, which covers legal privilege and confidentiality, and he contributed to and significantly rewrote my draft manuscript as it related to document retention (Chapter 8). These chapters were drawn both from his time working as investigator for my firm and from his studies at Brooklyn Law School. He also contributed significantly to the other chapters by acting as an editor and a sounding board for the other concepts in the book.

Chapter 7 of this book, on statement taking, was largely taken from my first book, *Private Investigator Entry Level (02E)*, and then reworked to fit in with the format of this book. I included this information again here because taking statements and obtaining declarations from witnesses is a critical documentation skill in cases involving litigation. In my view, no book on investigative documentation would be complete without a treatise on how to take statements, which can be used in court to impeach witnesses and even as stand-alone evidence in certain civil matters. I learned how to take verbatim statements from one of my business partners, Brendan Wells. I honed my skills obtaining declarations and affidavits over the years from work done mainly in employment litigation cases, including cases involving harassment, discrimination and retaliation. Statements may seem to some like kind of an afterthought in the context of the other principles described in this book, but I contend that they are an important subject matter in their own right nonetheless. In criminal defense investigations in particular, a thorough, well-written statement can prove integral for attorneys during cross-examination. A good statement elevates a well-documented investigation into an extremely well-documented investigation. It is the icing on the preverbial investigative cake.

The end result, I think, is a book on just about everything that an investigator needs to know regarding how to document an investigation in the private sector. Chapter 1 covers what I call the Five Principles of Investigative Documentation, and Chapter 2 details several misconceptions pertaining to investigative documentation. These two chapters are intended to set the stage for all of the information that follows on note-taking, running resumes, reports, statements and document retention. Each chapter is broken down into four or five sections that approximate the methods used to complete that particular documentary endeavor.

This book also contains an exhaustive appendix that many investigators will find useful in its own right. Beyond the section listing hundreds of abbreviations that investigators may find helpful when taking notes, I have included several examples of my firm's own reports—with names and other information changed to protect confidentiality. Readers may use these reports as templates for their own reports. The next section in the appendix includes an alphabetic stylebook, based on principles established at my firm as well as on styles utilized by the Associated Press and federal law enforcement agencies. This stylebook provides a quick tool to properly reference abbreviations, names, capitalization and numerals, among other topics. Finally, I have included several sample statements and declarations in the appendix to show what these documents are supposed to look like when they are completed.

One final note before we get to Chapter 1: this is not a book about how to conduct an investigation. There are better resources for that elsewhere. This is an advanced book on investigative documentation for people who already have the skills necessary to do an investigation. I have assumed, therefore, that readers will already know how to do an interview. For this reason, it is possible that I may have left out or glossed over some things that would paint the "complete picture" of how notes, running resumes, reports and statements fit into a larger investigation. People not experienced enough to recognize the importance of documentation may not be able to immediately connect the dots. Those who do, however, will see the quality of their investigations improve markedly and will ultimately be more successful in the field of private investigations by following the principles outlined in this book.

Philip A. Becnel IV

ACKNOWLEDGMENTS

A heartfelt thank you to everyone who made this book possible, particularly to Philip's wife, Melissa Aten, and Philip's father, Philip A. Becnel III, who both graciously sacrificed a great deal of their time to edit the manuscript in its earliest stages. We would also like to thank the partners and the employees of Dinolt Becnel & Wells Investigative Group for acting as sounding boards and for offering advice about some of the stickier areas of investigative documentation. This book would not have been possible without you!

CONTENTS

Page
Introduction vii

Chapter 1: Five Principles of Investigative Documentation 3
Chapter 2: Misconceptions Related to Documentation. 9
Chapter 3: Privilege and Confidentiality 15
Chapter 4: Note Taking. 21
Chapter 5: Running Resumes. 27
Chapter 6: Reports 35
Chapter 7: Statements 51
Chapter 8: Document Retention 63
Conclusion. 73

Appendix A: Investigative Acronyms/Abbreviations 77
Appendix B: Sample Reports. 85
Appendix C: Report Style Guidelines. 111
Appendix D: Sample Statements 137
Index 155

PRINCIPLES OF INVESTIGATIVE DOCUMENTATION

Chapter 1

FIVE PRINCIPLES OF INVESTIGATIVE DOCUMENTATION

A fundamental tenet of investigative documentation is that an investigator should document everything that he or she does–but that is not to say that everything needs to be documented in the exact same way. There are instances when a notation in the running resume is sufficient and when a report is not required. There are also instances when there is no need to add anything to the running resume and when a report is more appropriate. There are also instances when something must be documented in the running resume, in a report *and* with a statement. The only consistently-required form of documentation is notes: an investigator should take notes about everything. Even with notes though, there are instances when notes must be maintained, and there are instances when working notes may be destroyed. Before we learn about the specific methods of documentation, it is first important to understand under which circumstances to document and when certain types of documentation are not required.

I call these general rules for which medium to use to document a particular investigative task, and how long to keep these documents, the Five Principles of Investigative Documentation. I will discuss how to apply these principles in the chapters that follow; this chapter will deal with *when* to apply which principle. They are listed in the order that they would generally be applied during an investigation.

1. Take notes on everything that you do.

Again, the only consistently required form of documentation is notes. However, "notes" do not necessarily have to be *paper* notes. During background checks, the notes may be a working Word or other electronic document that an investigator uses to copy and paste pertinent information before it goes into a report. During surveillance or an interview that is being audio-recorded, notes may be the media file that captures those digital images or sounds, respectively. The term "notes" in this book is simply meant to connote contemporaneously recorded observations of any kind used in an investigation. Notes are so fundamental during investigations, because investigators often must remember the equivalent of several gigabytes of information during any given case, and too often it is impossible to recognize what is important until well into the investigation. Private investigators are essentially professional eye witnesses, preparing to testify from the minute they start an investigation. As such, they are subject to the same mistakes that regular witnesses make when it comes to memories that naturally fade with time and minds that subconsciously trick us into remembering events in a way that conforms to our expectations. Put simply, we must take note about everything, because we cannot trust our brains to remember these details for us later in the investigation.

2. Document every effort to contact a witness and all surveillance in the running resume.

Taking notes, however, is not enough by itself, because notes typically only have meaning to the person who wrote them. They are a memory aid, but they are inadequate for sharing information with others. But recall what was mentioned earlier: not every investigative task requires a formal report. It therefore stands to reason that, if we take notes about everything but do not write reports about everything, there must be some middle ground that we can employ to document useful information that does not find its way into our reports. This middle ground is the running resume. It is meant to capture and share information that falls in the chasm between notes and reports. It is sort of like a diary that an investigator keeps of certain investigative tidbits whose relevance is unknown at the time they were observed–but that might later be deemed relevant. Without the running resume, such information might otherwise languish in an investigator's notebook to be forgotten. Such tidbits include the time when a witness was contacted, a physical description of people encountered during the course of an investigation whose significance is unknown at the time of contact and the tag numbers and types of vehicles observed in a subject's driveway.

The general rule is that every effort to contact a witness must be documented in the case's running resume, whether the attempt was successful or not. This includes attempted phone calls and general observations made during surveillance. It is not necessary to add a notation to the running resume for online, non-telephonic research, such as when you use investigative databases to run background checks or to locate witnesses, as this information will go immediately into a report, which we will discuss next.

3. Prepare a report whenever there is a reasonable possibility that you will have to testify.

The most visible type of investigative documentation comes next: reports. If notes and running resumes are the bridges to reports, then reports are the single most important piece of any investigation and the primary tangible work product of the entire case. While other evidence sometimes rivals the importance of reports, such as a particularly compelling video file, the report is necessary to provide context to that evidence. A good report necessarily details the progress and the ultimate outcome of the investigation in a way that is meaningful to the client or to anyone else reading the report, and it provides a lasting record of the investigation that can be referenced (sometimes years) later. After notes and running resumes, investigators should prepare a report whenever there is a reasonable possibility that he or she will later have to testify. Since there are myriad reasons why an investigator may be called to testify, the broad rule is that reports are necessary whenever an investigative task is completed, whether it was successful or not. This rule includes all interviews, surveillance, background checks and undercover operations–basically anything that an investigator does.

4. Take verbatim statements from hostile or unhelpful witnesses; obtain declarations from friendly witnesses.

While reports may be the most important type of documentation, there are some other types of documentation that allow investigators to package evidence in a way that is above and beyond what is feasible in a report: statements, declarations and affidavits. The terms are not mutually exclusive—affidavits or declarations, for example, are essentially types of statements—but from a practical standpoint the format and the way in which the documents are collected are fundamentally different. Statements are the documents most likely to be discoverable (turned over to the opposition in litigation). The overarching purpose of all statements, whether affidavits, declarations or otherwise, is to perpetuate testimony and preserve memory. Statements lock witnesses into their accounts of what happened in a way that can be used later to refresh their recollections when they testify—or to impeach their credibility, should they change their stories prior to taking the stand. When to take what type of statement essentially boils down to whether the witness is cooperative or uncooperative, although other factors include the relevance of the witness to the case, the content of the witness's likely testimony and even the applicable jurisdiction of the case.

However, as a general rule, an investigator should take sworn verbatim statements from hostile or unhelpful witnesses immediately after the interview (i.e., before the report), but set up follow-up interviews with friendly witnesses to obtain sworn declarations or affidavits after the completion of the report. Obviously, when a witness is uncooperative enough to warrant a verbatim statement is a subjective evaluation—and witnesses who are uncooperative to the point of being hostile will likely refuse to provide a statement anyway. The section in the chapter on statement-taking titled "Take the best you can get under the circumstances" touches on these eventualities. In any case, a good rule of thumb is to ask yourself, "Does what this witness says support the client's case hypothesis?" If not, take a verbatim statement on the scene. We will discuss in greater detail the different types of statements and how to take them in Chapter 7.

5. Provide all of the case's documents to the client at the conclusion of the case—*or* have a document retention policy that decrees the maintenance of most records for at least five years.

No set of principles related to investigative documentation would be complete without addressing how long we must keep our records. Our reports and statements are provided to clients immediately after they are prepared, and the running resume may also be accessible to clients on an ongoing basis throughout the investigation, but other documents, like notes, are normally not turned over to clients automatically. Attorneys are bound to maintain copies of most of the records concerning their cases—including notes taken by investigators—for several years after the conclusion of the case. For lawyers, a case is considered closed when they cease representing the client, although a case does not truly end until a settlement or verdict is reached and the deadline for any potential appeal has passed. In other words, an attorney may withdraw from a case, only to be replaced by a new attorney, who may continue to represent the client for several more years. In serious criminal and civil matters, a case may not be completely resolved for up to a decade. The rules that lawyers must follow regarding document retention are complicated and vary by state, but altogether they are designed to preserve evidence and to facilitate the transfer of a case from one attorney to another.

Although investigators often work for attorneys and their investigative documentation is usually considered to be privileged attorney-client work product, most states do not require investigators to maintain their documents for any particular period of time. We maintain our documents to meet the individual requirements of the lawyers who hire us and also because maintaining our substantive records is often beneficial to the cases that we work long after we have completed the investigations. We are concerned about document retention, because good investigators are team players.

There are essentially two ways for investigative firms to address the issue of document retention: hand over all records to the attorneys at the conclusion of the case, or have a document retention policy that satisfies the need to preserve the evidence that we uncover in our investigations while facilitating the transfer of information to those who may work on our cases after we are through. If you hand over everything to the attorney–every page of notes, every e-mail, every draft report–then you do not need to worry about document retention; the impetus to maintain these records lies squarely on the shoulders of the attorney who hired you. You can skip right to Chapter 2, and you can skip reading Chapter 8 altogether.

If you are like most investigators, however, you are uncomfortable with the idea of handing over all your case documents to another person. For one thing, all of the substantive information in our notes and e-mails, for example, is already included in our running resumes, reports and statements, so collecting all of our notes and e-mails is an exercise in repetition. Also, our notes, taken during the heat of an investigation, can be a source of embarrassment later when removed from the context of the related reports. They often contain misspellings and allusions to leads that never materialized. Therefore, many investigative firms instead opt to maintain their own records consistent with their own document retention policies.

The most important feature of document retention is to have a stated, written policy that is communicated to every client and that sets out an exact time table and procedure for disposing of old case material. We recommend keeping records, reports, statements and any notes or e-mails concerning interviews for at least five years. Note that these guidelines are different than they are for attorneys, who sometimes must maintain their files for longer than five years, depending on the state where they practice. But investigators are not attorneys. In our experience, five years is sufficient to meet our own particular obligations. The procedures for document maintenance and retention will be discussed in detail in Chapter 8.

In the next chapter, we will discuss some of the common misconceptions related to investigative documentation.

Chapter 2

MISCONCEPTIONS RELATED TO DOCUMENTATION

Now that we have provided an overview of the basic requirements concerning when and what types of documentation are required in an investigation, we next want to dispel some of the common misconceptions. More than a decade ago, detectives carried around accordion style folders, with various subfolders labeled "notes," "reports," etc. Although we all still carry around similar appendages for easy access to our documents in the field, nowadays the bulk of our documentation is more than likely to be found on a computer network server. E-mails and files are sent and received right from our laptops and smart phones. Gone are the days of seemingly endless rows of metal filing cabinets; all of that information can now be kept on portable memory storage devices no bigger than the size of your thumb.

Also, there are now software programs and gadgets specifically designed to make it easier to document investigations. For example, our firm now uses a system called TrackOps, which catalogs cases in a very manageable, Web-based format, allowing us to upload photographs of our subjects and operate a slick running resume program. There are other, similar programs that are available, too. Many more investigators are now digitally recording interviews. The equipment available to record both audio and video aspects of an interview has become highly covert, and the digital space required to store this information has gotten cheap. Regardless of the specific system or devices used, technology has made it much easier to record, store, catalog, retrieve and share information about our cases, and this has somewhat changed our methods of documentation.

However, no technological innovation has supplanted the need for fundamental documentation practices that have evolved over the decades. For example, while using a digital recorder to record an interview may cause the reporting of that interview's content to be more accurate, an investigator still must summarize that information into a report in order to separate the relevant information from the remaining superfluous noise. Also, while running resume technologies allow users to prepare updates that can be easily shared with clients, the investigator still must type the information that goes into the updates, a process that is contingent on good note-taking in the field. As generous as technology has been to investigators, it has also served as the basis for two of the four most common myths related to documentation, which we will discuss below. The first two misconceptions, however, are as old as word processors.

Myth: Grammatical and other nonsubstantive mistakes do not matter in reports.

One of the most pervasive misconceptions is related to a failure to appreciate the important impact that words and punctuation have on our investigations and on our client's perceptions. It may seem laughable when stated in such a blatant manner, but many investigators implicitly believe that grammatical and other nonsubstantive mistakes do not really matter in reports. This is evident by the fact that errors are systemic in the investigative reports churned out by many investigators. Editing sloppy reports written by new investigators has at times been the bane of our existence, and those who have been unable to shape up have quickly found themselves working elsewhere, usually in another industry altogether. These individuals believe that having spell-check is a sufficient safeguard against spelling, punctuation and other errors and that clients and others do not notice mistakes that slip past these ubiquitous and imperfect software programs. Other investigators apparently do not even bother to use spell-check. The fact is that clients, judges, jurors and anyone else reading your reports *do* notice these types of mistakes, each of which serves to put a dent in your perceived professionalism. No client will ever send your report back to you with red lines all over it–but they will notice. The reason we know that they will notice is that *we* notice.

Besides just being sloppy and unprofessional, the words an investigator chooses to put in a report impact not only its credibility—they also have the potential to impact the report's intended meaning. The example provided in the Introduction is illustrative here. Sloppy note-taking could have cost a defendant his life. Take also the following example of an ambiguous, unclear report entry, taken from Philip's first book, *Private Investigator Entry Level (02E)*:

> When asked if John Adams ever mentioned Louisa Johnson's death to his co-workers, Washington said that it was odd how Adams mentioned that Johnson's parents **did** just one month earlier.

Below, see how the simple absence of the letter "e" in the word "died" completely alters the account of what the witness told the interviewing investigator.

> When asked if John Adams ever mentioned Louisa Johnson's death to his co-workers, Washington said that it was odd how Adams mentioned that Johnson's parents **died** just one month earlier.

The world is full of examples of ways in which seemingly minor typos have the potential to drastically alter a writer's intended meaning. Errors, no matter how small, have no place in any investigative report.

Myth: It is better *not* to document an investigation than to risk the documents becoming discoverable.

The second myth is that in some cases it is actually better *not* to document an investigation—in other words, to avoid notes and purposely not write reports—than to risk the documents becoming discoverable to the opposition. This myth is actually borne out of the practices of some law enforcement agencies to avoid producing exculpatory evidence that must later be turned over to the defense. It has also been perpetuated by some defense practitioners who are concerned about producing what is known as "reverse *Jencks*," which refers to the Supreme Court case and federal law that allows for the discoverability of previous statements of called witnesses in criminal cases. Without

---
* *Jencks v. United States*, 353 U.S. 657 (1957); *See also* 18 U.S.C. § 3500 ("The Jencks Act").

arguing about the ethical implications of these adverse but related philosophies, we submit that the concerns of law enforcement agencies related to when and how they choose to document their investigations are entirely irrelevant to private investigators and that the concerns regarding the production of reverse *Jencks* are overblown. Private investigators are not law enforcement agents, and therefore the rules for documenting a government investigation simply do not apply to us. Former police officers who leave their jobs to work in the private sector should leave their bad habits at their former agencies.

Reverse *Jencks* and the discoverability of investigation documentation in general is a valid concern with regard to statements, notes and e-mails sent to and from witnesses in criminal cases in jurisdictions allowing for reciprocal discovery. At the outset of a criminal defense investigation in any jurisdiction that utilizes the *Jencks* rules or similar reciprocal discovery, investigators must discuss with client defense attorneys a policy for documenting witness interviews to protect friendly, helpful witnesses from damaging impeachment, should they be called to testify. But reverse *Jencks* is a non-issue when it comes to documentation outside of criminal cases. When the *Jencks* rules do not apply, notes, running resumes and reports are work-product that clearly fall under the umbrella of attorney/client work product. These documents may become discoverable should you testify—which is why we care so much about their perfection—but the eventuality of testimony is not a valid excuse not to document; it is a validation of the necessity of solid, accurate documentation. There is no valid legal reason to purposely avoid documentation in any investigation in the private sector. Investigators must be careful what they write—but they must always write something.

Myth: E-mail is a sufficient means of documenting an investigation.

The third misconception relates to e-mail. The reasoning goes: because using e-mail in cases has become one of the standards for how we share information with our clients, why do I then need to write reports on top of my e-mails? Sending an e-mail, however, is never alone a sufficient means of documenting an investigation. The main problem is that e-mails, unlike reports, may be forwarded, deleted, altered or lost with the touch of button. Reports, on the other hand, are created, stored and shared in a way that makes a breach of protocol or confidentiality much less likely. Different operating systems and e-mail platforms have a way of altering the formatting of e-mails in a way that was not intended by the author. Also unlike reports, e-mail sent to and from witnesses is likely to be discoverable, even if you do not testify about its content. Simply put, e-mails are not a suitable medium for formal correspondence.

Communicating by e-mail does have its purpose. It is quick and effective for delegating tasks, confirming receipt of tasks, setting appointments and exchanging informal thoughts that do not fit readily in a report. But e-mails should never take the place of a formal report, and they should not be used to correspond with witnesses, except as a last resort. When e-mails are used to correspond with a client or others regarding a case, certain guidelines should be used to make the message of the e-mail clear and to make it easier for both the author and the recipient to find the message later. All e-mails to and from witnesses should be stored in a separate folder so that they cannot be inadvertently deleted and so that they can be easily turned over in the event they are discoverable. The subject of all e-mails sent during an investigation should include the case name, always followed by a statement summarizing the content of the e-mail. We capitalize the case name, but this is not a strict requirement. An appropriate subject of an e-mail might look like this:

Re: ABC BANK/ Efforts to schedule a meeting with William Harrison concerning a declaration

In the above example, ABC Bank is the name of the case, and the remainder of the header makes it clear what the e-mail is about. It would be very easy for someone to locate this e-mail later, by simply searching in an e-mail program for the terms "ABC Bank" or "William Harrison."

While we are on the subject of e-mail, it is also important to avoid slipping into informality with clients and others in the digital age. We have actually had complaints from clients when our investigators have been too informal in e-mails to witnesses. You should always err on the side of being too formal. For example, always include at the top of the e-mail's body the name of the intended recipient. This is very important in the smart phone age, when it is sometimes very difficult to determine on the portable device if an e-mail is intended for you or someone else copied on the same message. To avoid confusion, always name the recipient at the top of the e-mail (e.g., "Dear Mr. Harrison"), even for short messages and in instances when nobody else was copied on the e-mail. Last, avoid using slang or other informal abbreviations, even if you know the recipient very well. You have no control over what happens to that e-mail the second that you hit the send button, and the language of informality can sometimes be misinterpreted to imply bias during testimony concerning the messages.

Myth: Digital media do not require additional documentation.

The final misconception is that digital media, such as surveillance footage or audio-recorded interviews, do not require any additional documentation. This myth, like the one concerning e-mails, is one of the curses wrought by technology. The thinking goes that, since audio and digital recordings are more detailed than reports, the preparation of a report is repetitive and unnecessary. Proponents of this myth simply burn the file on a CD or DVD and hand it to their clients with no report or other documentation.

Digital media, however, are not analogous to reports, which act as summaries of relevant information; indeed, the incredible detail of digital media makes them most analogous to notes or statements, which, taken alone, are never sufficient documentation in themselves. Digital files (especially surreptitiously recorded ones) do not tell a client or a jury the context of how they were recorded. Also, like notes and verbatim statements, they are also full of superfluous information that is irrelevant to the case. Investigators should never make their clients sift through this information to determine what is and is not relevant. This task falls under the purview of an investigator's job.

To summarize, digital media that are relevant to an investigation, like good notes or statements, only form the basis of reports, which give the other media specific meaning in the investigation. Digital media that is *not* relevant to the investigation, like irrelevant notes, may be documented solely in the running resume—but they must always be documented in one manner or the other. An audio or video file is never enough.

Chapter 3

PRIVILEGE AND CONFIDENTIALITY

With all documentation of an investigation come questions of confidentiality and the client's privilege that communications made by and through investigators remain safe from adversarial discovery. For centuries, courts have recognized the necessity of confidentiality between clients and the attorneys that they hire. The concept is simple: guarantees of confidentiality facilitate the free flow of information between clients and their legal representatives. Without confidentiality and privileged communications, clients would be rightfully nervous to share any detrimental information with their legal representatives for fear that the court would one day require that it be turned over to their adversary. The rule for attorneys is so sacrosanct that the American Bar Association's Model Rules of Professional Conduct require attorneys to maintain absolute confidentiality of client information, unless the client specifically consents to its disclosure or in other very limited situations.[†]

The rule is just as important when applied to investigators, who by their very nature are tasked with handling and collecting confidential information and communicating the results of their investigations securely to their clients. Just as with attorneys, investigators undertaking the representation of a client involved in litigation or potential litigation of any kind are expected to maintain the utmost levels of confidentiality. This responsibility becomes even more significant when investigators document their investigations. Understanding the nature of privileged communication, its scope and how to maintain that privilege is an imperative part of investigation documentation. Proper un-

---

[†] Model Rules of Prof'L Conduct R. 1.6 (2010).

derstanding of the fundamentals of confidentiality in documentation will help the investigator to protect clients' interests and ensure secure communication.

While this is an area that is often best left to attorneys with jurisdiction-specific knowledge of confidentiality, understanding the basics of how the privilege works is important for any investigator tasked with documenting the results of his or her investigations. The most important thing for investigators to understand about confidentiality is that it only exists when working for attorneys who are engaged in litigation or potential legal action. Investigators may swear to their individual clients that they will not share information, but absent an attorney and a legal issue, courts can require that any documentation you produce be turned over to the opposition in the event of a legal action.

The attorney-client privilege extends to investigators.

The attorney-client privilege extends to private investigators who are hired by attorneys in order to provide services in connection with legal representation.[‡] This rule was formed in response to clients' needs to hire investigators to render services that an attorney may be unprepared or ill-equipped to provide during the course of representation. An example of this is when an employment law attorney needs help tracking down and interviewing a former co-worker of her client who has since moved out of the state. The investigator would therefore need to speak to the client in order to gather information to be able locate the co-worker and to learn the nature of the information that the co-worker is believed to have, including whether or not that employee might have information detrimental to the client.

If confidentiality did not extend to the investigator, any of these communications—including any document sent to the attorney following the interview—could be susceptible to discovery. In effect, the investigator would be working for the client's adversary. Courts and state bar associations have recognized this dilemma and, recognizing the necessity of investigators in certain cases, have extended confidentiality from attorneys to their investigators.

* As a special note. A confidential relationship can be put in peril, even in cases of ongoing litigation if a non-attorney client pays an investigator directly. Therefore, an investigator should caution attorneys

---

[‡] See *United States v. Kovel*, 296 F.2d 918, 921–22 (2d. Cir. 1961) (establishing privilege for agents of attorneys during legal representation); *see also United States v. McPartlin*, 595 F.2d 1321, 1337 (7th Cir. 1979) (stating that investigators can be agents of attorneys and therefore convey confidentiality).

to always submit payments, lest they risk losing the privilege of confidentiality.

The scope of confidentiality is limited.

Simply because the right to confidentiality has been extended to investigators does not, however, mean that every document that an investigator produces will forever be hidden away from the eyes of an adversary. The most important thing to keep in mind is that confidentiality is only extended to a private investigator's internal discussions and communications and those discussions with the represented client and the attorneys working on the case. No privilege exists between the investigator and a third party, nor does it exist in communications outside the scope of the reason for legal representation. Nevertheless, it is important to understand the scope of the client's right to confidentiality to avoid situations in which you may believe that a document is covered by the attorney-client privilege, but in fact it is not. Let's take the example of a large corporate accounting firm that hires a private investigative firm to provide criminal background checks on all potential new hires. After six months of providing these background checks and the requisite reports covering the results that follow, the accounting firm is sued for negligence in hiring after several of its new accountants embezzled a client's money. Here, even if the accounting firm's attorneys were the ones to hire the private investigators and supervised their activities, there would be no confidentiality to the background check reports. Upon demand, in the majority of jurisdictions, the investigator would be required to turn over the documents as discovery.

This is because only information that is rendered by the private investigator to attorneys for services in connection with ongoing or potential litigation can be considered privileged and confidential.[§] Here, the background checks were provided as an employment service and not in connection with ongoing or pending litigation. The scope of the investigator's confidentiality is limited to those cases in which he or she is providing services for a specific legal need on a specific case. However, as investigators, we are often brought in by our clients prior to the institution of legal action against another party. As such, the privilege extends to our investigations made in specific preparation for

---

§ *See* In Re Human Tissue Prods. Liab. Litig., 255 F.R.D. 151, 161–62 (D.N.J. 2008) (finding that investigators must be providing services to attorneys relating directly to a legal issue to invoke privilege).

litigation. The bigger question for confidentiality of investigative documentation revolves around the way in which investigators handle the documentation.

Confidentiality must be maintained.

When an issue of confidentiality of an investigator's reports arises, one of the first things that courts will examine is the manner of the communication and how it was transmitted to an attorney. This is the most important part for the documenting investigator, as this is where your actions can directly impact whether or not confidentiality exists.

Confidentiality exists because we expect it to exist; courts recognize this in any evaluation of the attorney-client privilege. For instance, if you had a secret that you expected a friend to keep and that you did not want others to know, you would likely bring the friend aside to a private area and tell that friend about your secret. If you did not care whether or not others knew, you might just walk up to the friend as he stood in a large group of others and loudly announce what you had to say. Just as you would take the friend alone to a private place to discuss the secret, it is likewise important to institute measures to maintain confidentiality in investigative documentation. Often, investigators think that they are safe simply by putting "Privileged Attorney-Client Work Product" as a header on every page of an investigative report. While this is an important step in delineating the intention of the investigator and the attorney to keep the matter confidential, it may not confer confidentiality standing alone. This is particularly true if there are other detrimental factors. For instance, if you were to walk up to that same group of friends, look at one person and loudly announce, "I have a secret and you can't tell others"—but then you loudly belted out your secret for all to hear, surely you cannot expect the disclaimer to mean that your secret was not heard by others.

This is why it is important to institute a formal policy for transmitting information and documentation intended to be kept confidential to attorneys in a secure and consistent manner. All investigative reports intended to be kept privileged should include the header "Attorney Work Product." E-mails to attorneys with investigative reports attached and other sensitive information should be forwarded directly and solely to the attorney working on the case. If you are working with a law firm that employs multiple attorneys, it would be best to make sure that you are not sending the e-mail out to dozens of attorneys in a particular division, but only those attorneys directly responsible for that case. Supervising investigators in your firm can be copied with investigative reports and client communications; however, it is wise to keep it to one investigator with the most direct supervision over you or the case. Absent a specific instruction from the attorney, reports should never be sent to third parties. While attorneys may encourage you to send your reports directly to their clients, you should be aware that sending reports to e-mail accounts set up by an employer or a school is not advisable. Often these accounts are under the control of a third party, and as a result, may be seen as a breach of confidentiality, making those communications discoverable by adversaries.

Imagine what would happen if you were investigating a workplace discrimination case on behalf of a plaintiff client and the client wanted you to send all of your reports to his e-mail address set up through the very employer that he wishes to sue. A judge may not take long in determining that there could be no expectation of confidentiality if the employer looked into this e-mail account and retrieved every report you wrote in the case. You should discuss maintenance of confidentiality with an attorney any time he or she asks you to send e-mailed reports and communications directly to a client.

These same rules also hold true for oral communications. Take for instance, a criminal defense investigation. The attorney has hired you to investigate a homicide case, and you arrive in court for a hearing. At the close of the hearing, the attorney asks you to go back and speak to the client to determine who else may have been at the scene of the murder. You go to lock-up and engage the client in a conversation that is overheard by five other inmates awaiting hearings and two guards. Even though you may follow the most meticulous policy to maintain confidentiality in drafting your follow-up report with the attorney, you may have just sacrificed any confidentiality you had by having that conversation in an open environment audible to others. In some jurisdictions, due to what is held to be a destruction of confidentiality on the issue in question, the prosecution may even be able to discover any subsequent information you obtained from witnesses resulting from that conversation.

When attorneys and their clients expect information gleaned by an investigator to be kept confidential, investigators must always be vigilant in instituting the most guarded policies to maintain that confidentiality. This responsibility is most important in the proper preparation of documentation for all investigations.

Chapter 4

NOTE TAKING

It is not feasible to prepare reports or add to a case's running resume while out in the field. Although smart phones and other wireless instruments make it possible to perform some level of digital documentation in the field, the reality is that it is exceedingly difficult to write reports or the like from your car or in the presence of witnesses. Therefore, the first practical application of documenting any type of evidence during an investigation in the field starts with taking notes. As discussed in Chapter 1, an investigator should take notes about everything he or she does, including interviews and surveillance. As a practical matter, an investigator may not always be able to take notes during an activity, such as during a mobile surveillance or an interview with an uncooperative witness (who might be spooked at the sight of a pen and notepad), but he or she should always jot down everything promptly after-the-fact to maintain a clear record of the event. Sometimes investigators opt instead to maintain notes during mobile surveillance by using an audio-recording device.

In this chapter, we will introduce five tips for effective note-taking, to be discussed in detail in the sections that follow.

1. Always bring along at least two pens and a clean legal pad.

Starting with what may be obvious to some readers, an investigator should always bring along at least two pens and a clean legal pad anytime that he or she is actively working on a case. Pens run out of ink, and it is always important to have a backup. Also, it does no good to bring a notepad if you are going to run out of paper in the middle of an interview. Know how long your interview will likely last, and bring along twice as much paper as you think you need. Be sure also to have a reporter-style notepad (usually 4" by 8") or similar hand-held recording instrument in your vehicle and at home, even when you are not working, as witnesses have a way of calling after hours when you are not on the case, so to speak. You must always use a clean sheet of paper and include the date regarding every separate event. Each page should only record information about one subject; never write about two different cases on the same sheet of paper. While this may be bad for the environment, it is important that notes be kept in the folder of the related case and that confidential information from one case not comingle with the files of another.

2. Learn to listen and observe first, and then take notes afterward.

The next step of good note-taking is learning to listen and observe first, and then to take notes afterward. This is important because taking notes creates the potential for an investigator's attention to be diverted from what is being investigated. An investigator who has his or her nose buried in the notepad cannot, for example, also observe an interview subject's behavior, which could give clues regarding the subject's veracity. This problem is largely averted by taking notes immediately after–not during–the observation. During an interview, for example, the investigator asks a question, listens to and observes the response, and then records those observations in the notepad.

To provide another example, during an undercover operation–when taking notes would obviously be impossible–the investigator should take notes immediately upon leaving the location of the operation. The same concept applies during surveillance: never attempt to write while driving. Instead jot down the notes when you come to a complete stop and when there is no more meaningful activity to observe–or use an audio recorder. Whatever the particular case or the method used to document it in the field, the investigator should be careful not to allow the documentation process to get in the way of the investigator's primary mission, which is to observe and to be prepared to testify about those observations.

3. Think proactively and ask the right questions.

The best investigative documentation comes out of the best interviewing and note-taking. Often, when we complete an interview with that hard-to-reach witness, we find ourselves returning to write up the investigative report only to find out that we did not clarify the year in which he left his most recent job. The devil is in the details when it comes to investigation. Understanding what details are going to be needed later while you are actually conducting the interview makes it much easier to write the most thorough report possible.

To be able to fully investigate a case, we must be able to capture the proper details that will allow us to generate additional evidence. Every investigator should remember four subjects that should instinctively be followed up on during an interview: dates, times, full names and proper names. For example, in an industrial equipment products liability case, a witness may inform you that she was present when "Dana," a co-worker, was injured using the same equipment and that her supervisor took her to the hospital. You should instinctively follow up by getting Dana's full name, the full name of the supervisor and the name of the hospital. In another case, a witness might tell you that he worked only until "the other month," or that he used to leave work "in the afternoon." You should follow up on both of these answers immediately by inquiring for specific dates and times. The issue of proper names will often come up with places or businesses. Imagine that a witness tells you she saw a witness leave to go to a bar immediately after an event. It logically follows that we would want the name of the bar. It is also important to date the notes themselves to indicate what time the interview or other investigative activity took place. For the best investigators, these practices become instinctual.

But don't keep your follow-up questions limited to the above-mentioned four areas. People are often very unclear in conversation; we often expect people to understand what we mean and to have the same background knowledge as we do. For investigators interviewing new witnesses, this is hardly ever the case. Keep an eye out for any vague statements, particularly of people, places and things. A witness who tells you that something happened, "over on the other side," of a building should immediately trigger you to ask her for a description of where, specifically, she means to say that the event occurred.

With the right questions and an ear for thorough, proactive interviewing, you will have all of the information you need in front of you when you sit down to write up the final interview report.

4. Develop your own system for abbreviations.

Notes are primarily a memory aid for the investigator. For this reason, details sufficient enough to trigger recall are more important than how intelligible they are to others. In fact, investigators sometimes find that it helps for their notes to be largely encoded with their own particular shorthand. In the event that their notes become discoverable, this makes it harder for the opposing counsel to later decode them and use them against you. All investigators should develop their own system abbreviations in their notes, as this saves time in the field and helps make the events clear later when translated for writing the reports. Take the following example:

Q: Criminal?
A: + ADW FFC 1999 C & AWIK PW 2001 NP

In this example, the question is meant to refer to a commonly-asked question: have you ever been arrested? The response indicates that, yes (+) the person indicated an arrest for assault with a deadly weapon in Fairfax County in 1999, which was a conviction (C), and also for assault with intent to kill in Prince William's County in 2001—a case that was dismissed or "*nolle prossed*" (NP). There is an extensive list of abbreviations that you may find useful for taking notes in Appendix A of this book.

Keep in mind though that most of these abbreviations should *only* be used while taking notes—not in the running resume or in reports or statements. The reason for this is that note-taking is intended primarily to refresh an investigator's recollection of events to facilitate more accurate running resumes and reports. The abbreviations that the author chooses to use, therefore, are very personal and subjective. The abbreviations that one investigator chooses to use may not mean anything to another investigator. Running resumes, reports and statements, on the other hand, are shared with other people, who presumably did not actually witness the events. For this reason, abbreviations in reports, running resumes and statements may be misunderstood and have the potential to create confusion that could harm the case. Only very common and well-known abbreviations should ever be used in running resumes and reports. At our firm, the suggested abbreviations in the appendix that are italicized may be used in running resumes but not in reports, and the bolded abbreviations may be used in both running resumes and reports. The only abbreviations that should be used in statements are ones that the witness used at the time that the statement was taken.

In summary, running resumes must be fully understood by fellow investigators, while reports must be fully understandable to lay persons who may not be familiar with abbreviations or other investigative jargon. Notes must only be understandable to the person who wrote them, although they must be factually consistent with all the other documentation in the case that follows. However, to the extent that they are understandable to other people, notes must be written in a way that makes their meaning clear. Having an established system of abbreviations makes misinterpretation less likely to happen.

5. Review your notes immediately after the activity.

The last note-taking tip for investigators is to review and clarify notes immediately after the activity. This is a little different than the advice above, because here we are advocating that—after the interview, surveillance or other investigative activity—the investigator then read the notes in their entirety and make sure they are completely consistent with the investigator's recollection of what was said or observed. The reason this is important is that sometimes we misunderstand things that a subject said at one point during an interview, but then that same issue is clarified later in the same interview. Also, we may jot down during surveillance that a subject turned down one particular street, only to later discover that we wrote down the wrong street. These misunderstandings must be corrected in the notes to reflect what actually occurred. It is best to perform this exercise very soon after the activity, when your memory is still fresh about the events. Relatedly, notes taken in a haphazard manner may be confusing or appear contradictory to a subsequent report, which can negatively affect the case.

Always take the time to carefully review all of your notes. Add things that are missing, based upon your recollection. Correct things that are inconsistent with your recollection by placing a single line through the things that were recorded incorrectly and writing down the information that is correct in the spaces between the lines. Do not be concerned about how this may look to the opposing counsel or to a juror if you are later testifying about the activity detailed in the notes. It is far easier to explain a correction than to explain why your notes are inaccurate. Do not completely scratch out anything in the notes, however, as a skilled attorney will quickly seize on this "unknown" and try to make the deletion into something more significant than it really is.

After you have carefully reviewed and corrected your notes, drive a staple through them. You are now ready for the running resume.

Chapter 5

RUNNING RESUMES

A running resume is a shared document or software system, sort of like a journal, where investigators working on a given case provide brief status updates concurrent with each effort made to complete the case's individual tasks. The case's tasks include things like interviewing a particular witness, performing background checks on individuals or conducting surveillance during a fixed period of time. The running resume should be maintained by the investigative firm, not the individual investigator. Running resumes are ultimately collaborative documents. Their main value lies in information easily shared by multiple investigators on the team and with the case manager. They may or may not be sent to clients, depending on the policy of the investigative firm.

Our firm shares its running resumes with clients using TrackOps, a computer software program that keeps a running resume for work tasks. Entries are completed in this system by going to the case updates tab and adding a public update, which clients can then access by logging directly into our system using a Web interface. Permission protocols are set in advance so that clients can only access their own cases. We have customized our update categories so that there is a drop-down menu with the names of different types of updates followed by our individual investigators' initials in parentheses. This is to make it clearer to our clients which investigator wrote which update. The particular system and format of a running resume is less important than the fact that the information is maintained and shared by the investigators on the team and with the case manager.

A running resume will never be discoverable, although it may be subpoenaed in the event that the firm is not covered by the legal privilege of an attorney. Again, there is no specific requirement to offer a case's running resume to a client, although there is really no reason not to do so. Irrespective of whether it is shared with the client or not, a running resume allows the lead investigator or case manager to easily check on the status of each active investigation and also provides insurance that each task is documented properly. Ultimately, as the investigation progresses, a running resume becomes a chronological record of all of the happenings of the investigation. Because it is all in one location, it is easy for the case manager to see all of the steps taken to achieve the goal of the investigation. While this does not negate the need for meetings and other communication during the investigation, it does make the process of managing an investigation much easier, and it provides a lasting record of the case for later reference. Investigators also can and should draw on the information in the running resume as they are later preparing their reports concerning the investigation.

Here is a simple example of a running resume entry taken from our firm. The names and other information have been changed in the documentary examples throughout this book to protect confidentiality. This update is regarding a simple telephone call to a witness.

> I called Franklin Pierce at 301-555-3072 and left VM. A female voice on greeting stated that I had reached the cellular phone of "Jane." Note that Pierce's g/f is believed to be Jane Appleton, who may reside at 1715 U St., Apt. 3, NW, Washington, DC 20009.

As you can see from this example, even the simple task of making a phone call to a witness yields potentially valuable information. In this case, our investigator noted that the greeting for the telephone may indicate that the number belongs to the subject's girlfriend.

Now, let us get into the weeds.

1. Add a notation to the running resume for all interviews, attempted interviews and surveillance.

As important as running resumes are during investigations, not every investigative activity must be recorded in the running resume. What does and does not require a running resume entry depends a lot on if or when the relevant information will later be put into an investigative report. We will discuss reports and how to prepare them in greater detail in Chapter 5, but first we need to outline the requirements for when reports are required, as this information relates directly to the requirements of running resumes.

All interviews and surveillance automatically require the completion of a formal investigative report. Attempted interviews only require the completion of a report in the event that the investigator definitively and finally failed to achieve the interview—in other words, if the subject refused to cooperate or if exhaustive efforts to find the person failed.

Research requires a report unless the results of the research are implicitly included within the goal of a broader given task. For example, research intended only to locate a witness so that he or she may be interviewed does not necessarily require a report, since that witness's whereabouts would be included in the report concerning the interview.

With these rules in mind, the purpose of a running resume is to bridge the gap between notes and reports. For this reason, some of the most important pieces of information that are included in the running resume are the so-called "failures" of the investigation—for example, the missteps taken before contact was made with a difficult witness and the hours spent on a surveillance assignment when no seemingly meaningful activity was observed. Some of this information may or may not find its way into a report eventually, but in any case it must be documented beyond the mere notes that the investigator took in the field. The general rule is to add a notation to the running resume for all interviews, attempted interviews and surveillance. Research generally does not require a running resume entry, although there are some exceptions. Research done solely to further another task—like to find a subject for an interview—should be documented in the running resume. At my firm, the results of such research are also added to the relevant subject's profile in our running resume system. Research done for the sole purpose of gathering information, such as for a background check, does not need to be added to the running resume.

Below is an example of a running resume entry that demonstrates how research to locate a witness was documented in one of our cases. The entry relates to a homeless witness who, after our investigator left cards for him at a local homeless shelter, ultimately agreed to come into our office for an interview:

Warren Harding called my office today from 571-555-0653. The caller ID indicates this number belongs to "Florence DeWolf." I was in an interview at the time that the call came, so Harding left me a VM, saying that he heard that I had been looking for him and that he wants me to do something for him. He said that he was out of town for a little while, but that he is now back. He told me that he would try me again later today.

I called Harding back at the 571 number several times, but each of my calls was put into a generic VM. I will continue trying to call him.

Research indicates that the number is a land line phone that belongs to Florence Kling DeWolf at 1038 S. Frederick St., Apt. 101, Arlington, VA 22204.

Harding later called me back from 703-555-9711. The caller ID indicates that this number belongs to Helen Taft. Harding told me that he would meet me at my office in an hour.

Notice that there are references to database research concerning the telephone numbers the witness was using to contact our office. This degree of detail is not necessary for a report, but it could assist our investigators in locating this witness again in the future.

2. Update your running resume daily.

It stands to reason that for running resumes to be helpful to the investigation, the entries must be entered as soon as possible after the activity that they describe. My firm requires investigators to enter their update into the system no later than 10 a.m. the next day for activity that occurred on the previous day. It is easy to become complacent when it comes to this important step, because investigators are too often already focused on their next task. Therefore, updating the running resume must become a part of your daily routine and seen as an integral part to the investigation.

Next is a second example of a running resume entry, this one about a day's efforts to locate a difficult witness:

At around 10 a.m. this morning I attempted to locate and interview Mary Morstan at 1737 Glen Echo Rd., Nashville, TN 37215. This is a small green house, perhaps a studio or a one-bedroom. On the mailbox in white paint is inscribed the name "Morstan." There was a brown puppy running around loose in the front yard, which is not completely enclosed.

At that time I spoke to a BM, about 10-years old, who went and got a BM in his late teens or early 20s. This man, who was about 5'8" tall and wore corn rows in his hair, told me that he is Morstan's brother. He said that Morstan does not live there anymore and that he does not know where Morstan stays. He then called Morstan on his own cell phone and handed me the phone. The call went to VM, so I left a detailed message for her to call me. Her brother advised me that Morstan was probably still sleeping, but that he would have her call me. I then asked the man for a number where I could also try to reach his sister directly, and he provided Morstan's number as 615-555-9315.

I waited several hours at my motel for Morstan to call, and when I did not hear from her I tried the number provided by the brother. The number was disconnected.

I then returned to the house around 3:30 p.m. and again knocked on the door. This time an elderly BF came out of the side door of the house and introduced herself as Morstan's mother. She was about 5'4" tall with a thin build and scars on her arms. She told me that she does not know where her daughter stays either. I asked her to confirm the number that Morstan's brother had given me earlier, and (after looking at the number Morstan's brother had given me) she wrote the number down as 615-555-9316. She said that she would also relay a message for Morstan to call me.

I then left Morstan a detailed VM at 615-555-9316, asking for her to return my call. The greeting on this number is unintelligible, but it does not sound like a female's voice. I left another VM at this number later in the evening.

It is mostly likely that this number too is incorrect and that Morstan is still using 703-555-1785, the number Det. Sherlock Holmes used to reach her.

The above information was never put into a formal report, because we eventually interviewed the witness. The reason why this update does not mention the interview is that it was recorded about 10 hours before the interview occurred, which was on the following morning. It was later deemed to be irrelevant that both the witness's brother and mother had provided false information about her whereabouts. But at the time of this running resume entry, this was all the information that was deemed to be important to the task of locating this witness.

3. Always include biographical information about the subject or subjects of the update.

Next, as the above examples should illustrate, the real value of a running resume is in the details. A running resume must include sufficient detail in the individual notations—including exact times and environmental data. It is often the case that, hidden within the activities deemed at the time to be failures, investigators later find the clues necessary to ultimately achieve the desired goal of the investigation. These details include biographical data about the people we interact with during our assignments, such as their height, weight, hair color, etc. They also include the descriptions and tag numbers of vehicles observed around the vicinity of the buildings that we observe during surveillance—even if it is possible that those vehicles have nothing to do with the issue under investigation. Often a running resume entry will only concern a telephone call, but even with this brief task there are important details that must be documented. For example, did anyone answer the phone or did the voice-mail pick up the call? Was a name mentioned in the voice-mail greeting, or was it just a generic greeting? All of these facts may provide important clues to solve important problems later in the case.

Here is an example of a running resume entry concerning a surveillance case:

> We again began our surveillance at ABC Bank, located at 2017 15th St. NW, Washington, DC, at about 7:50 a.m. but did not see any activity until about 9:15 a.m. During part of this time I went to see if we could p/u Mary Bellamy from ABC Bank's main office at 300 14th St., NW, Washington, DC 20005. However, I did not observe her there.

At 9:15 a.m., Bellamy pulled into the mouth of the alley at 2017 15th St. where she has been seen on previous occasions parking her car. She was driving a white Mercedes SUV with DC Tag# DH 5570. The vehicle had some damage on its right front bumper. She is described as a WF, about 5'5" tall, 130 pounds, with straight, brown hair. She was wearing a gray pantsuit and a red scarf.

Bellamy returned to her car a few minutes later and was observed backing out of the alley at around 9:22 a.m., driving SB on 15th St., WB on I St., NB on 18th St. and EB on the access road adjacent to K St. There she pulled into an alley and left her car at the mouth of the alley where it comes out on 18th St. There we temporarily lost sight of her. However, we later observed her walking from the direction of 18th St. and K St. She then got into her vehicle and began to pull out of the alley, but then she reversed her vehicle and returned to the alley.

We then observed Bellamy exit her vehicle and walk into 1702 K St., NW, Washington, DC 20006 at around 9:50 a.m. She remained inside of this building for several minutes and then exited, returning to her vehicle with a box in her hands. We shot some video of her leaving this building.

Bellamy then drove NB on 18th St., EB on K St., and NB on 15th St., where she parked in front of 2017 15th St., NW. She remained at this location until approximately 10:25 a.m., when she made a U-turn on 15th St. and headed SB on 15th, EB on H St., SB on 14th St., and WB on New York Ave., making a U-turn at the end of the road and pulling into the parking garage located on the south side of the block of 301 14th St., NW.

We continued observing this building until 11:43 a.m. for any additional signs of Bellamy, but we did not see her again. We then signed off the surveillance.

Even during surveillance when the investigator may have been able to capture an image of the subject, it is important to also include these details in the running resume, where they can be readily accessed by other investigators on the team without having to review all of the digital media. In this case, another team of investigators was ready to take over the surveillance on the following day, so the information was vital to the continuity of the investigation.

4. Send updates to clients when a task was completed successfully or if it was a definitive failure.

Finally, while running resumes are principally for internal use by the investigative firm, they have the added benefit of providing excellent updates to clients before it is feasible for an investigator to prepare a report. At our firm, investigators always send the updates to clients in this manner when a task was completed successfully or if it was a definitive failure. In both of these scenarios, the running resume entry is later followed by a formal report, but the running resume entry can be sent to the client much faster. Our running resume system (Track-Ops) allows us to e-mail such significant updates directly to clients from the system. This is done by clicking on a link on the right of the update, which then prompts the investigator to click on the update's recipients (the case manager and the clients, who were added when the case was initially set up) and send the entire update as an e-mail.

Once a running resume update has been sent to a client, a report can be prepared anytime within the next 48 hours. Remember though that, although running resumes are not expressly written for clients, the entries still must be professional and should not contain too much technical jargon. As we have already discussed, certain abbreviations are okay in the running resume, but others are bound to confuse lay people and even other investigators. Both the italicized and bolded abbreviations in Appendix A of this book are acceptable for use in the running resumes at my firm. Those that are not italicized or bolded are only acceptable for use in the investigator's own notes. Each notation must also be grammatically correct, including complete sentences and proper punctuation.

Now that you have completed a running entry regarding your investigative task, it is time to write your report.

Chapter 6

REPORTS

All of our efforts to take accurate and detailed notes and to further document our investigations in the running resume are ultimately geared toward helping us write better reports, which are the single most important thing we produce as investigators. When you really boil down the business of private investigation, we observe things and we write about those things in our reports, which we then sell to our clients. In some cases, we may go beyond writing a report—we may take a sworn declaration from a witness (to be discussed in Chapter 7), and we may even testify—but even these important tasks would be incomplete without a solid, well written report to refresh our memories and buttress our credibility. Not everyone is a great writer, although those who cannot write reasonably well tend not to last long as private investigators. Still, there are things that everyone can do to make their reports more effective. Here are 10 guidelines that we use at my firm for writing effective reports:

1. Use a template and a style guidebook.

Broadly speaking, there are three types of reports—preliminary reports, status reports and concluding reports—although what they are called is not as significant as what they contain. The preliminary report in any form is essentially what outlines the nature of the investigation and may also implicitly include the case's goal or problem that needs to be solved. In *Private Investigator Entry Level (02E),* Philip wrote that, in the private sector, preliminary reports may be prepared by a principal of the firm in some instances, but that more often they are actually prepared by the client. We have actually come to reconsider this statement. We now think that, for private investigators, the document most analogous to a preliminary report is a contract, to the extent that it acts as a memorandum of understanding regarding what the client hopes will be accomplished during the investigation. As this book is not about contracts, we are going to focus here solely on what are broadly called status reports and concluding reports. The major difference between a status and a concluding report is that a status report is limited to information that is relevant to only one task—an interview, attempted interview, a background check on an individual or surveillance during a fixed period of time—while a concluding report summarizes information across multiple tasks. Use a template that is designed for the type of report and the underlying investigative endeavor. As stated above, all reports prepared while working on behalf of an attorney should include the phrase "Attorney Work Product" in the header of the report. This is essential to protect the privileged nature of the communication in the event that the report is inadvertently released to a third party or an adversary wishes to make it the focus of discovery.

You will find an example of a concluding report and several different status reports in Appendix B of this book. These examples can easily be modified to create templates that your firm can employ in its own investigations.

Also, have an established guidebook for the consistent style that the writing in your reports should follow. Should a witness's job title be capitalized? What is the correct way to write a date in your reports? While your style may vary, what is most important is having a consistent, stated policy. We have included our guidebook in Appendix C of this book to address the way that we have opted to answer these and other common questions. In this guidebook you can quickly look up the proper way to write about many of the things that we encounter in our investigations, including how to use numerals and proper names. While these guidelines may not fit exactly with the practices of every investigative firm, it is important that investigators prepare all of their reports using the same set of rules, because clients notice when different reports do not follow the same style and format. Discrepancies indicate that you do not pay attention to the details, which is not the message that you want to send to readers of your reports.

2. Name the report in a way that it can be easily identified later.

Although this may seem obvious, name the report in a way that it can be easily identified later, and save it repeatedly while working on it to avoid losing data. You would be surprised how common it is for novice investigators to name their reports simply "Report" or "New Microsoft Word Document." Reports that are not properly named will invariably be lost. It is therefore imperative to have a system in place for naming documents in a manner that makes it easier to retrieve them later. The year should be listed first, followed by the month and the day both in a two-digit format. This is to make a list of reports for the same case chronological when they are stored in the same digital folder. After the date, the investigator should name it in the most straightforward manner possible. The name should succinctly describe what is in the report. Examples of how to name the sample reports included in Appendix B might be:

2010_12_23_Kines Hal interview

2008_07_12_Murdoch Ian interview

2009_01_30_Devlin, Moriarty and Legrand final report

2006_06_19_Gutman Casper surveillance

On a related note, it is also fairly common for investigators to complain about losing half-completed reports after a power outage or similar mechanical malfunction. For this reason, investigators should get into the habit of manually saving their reports every several minutes while they are writing them.

3. Clearly indicate the report's author and recipients.

Now that you are using the correct template for your report and have it named properly, it is important that the report clearly name its author and recipients. This too may seem very basic, but in many cases, particularly for law firms, there are sometimes several attorneys and legal assistants involved in any given case. There may also be multiple investigators working on the same case. When most of the contact between the client and the firm goes through the case manager, attorneys and other clients may become confused about who actually performed the investigation detailed in any given report. In fact, sometimes when working for larger law firms, the case manager interacts principally with an associate attorney and rarely with the law firm's partner, who is overseeing the case. The investigator therefore may be separated by two degrees of separation from the report's primary customer–and by three degrees of separation from the law firm's client, who is ultimately bankrolling the investigation. For this reason, it must be clear from the header of the report who wrote it and who needs to read it. In the templates that our firm uses, each report has only one primary recipient: this is the primary requester of the information contained in the report.

Here is an example of a header from one of our reports:

INVESTIGATIVE REPORT

DATE: DECEMBER 23, 2010

FROM: JAMES ROCKFORD (JSR); JAKE GITTES (JJG)

TO: JACK WILLIAMS

CC: PAT CHAMBERS

CASE NAME: ABC BANK (01-00121)

Keep in mind, however, that Jack Williams in this report is not necessarily the highest level employee at the law firm; he is simply the person most likely to read and act on the information in the report. It may be an associate or a legal assistant. Beyond these guidelines, however, whenever there is a question of who should be listed as the report's primary recipient, it should always go to the more senior of the two individuals. In the CC section of the template, all of the remaining recipients should be listed, including the case manager of the investigative firm. At our firm, we separate the names with semicolons.

The name of the author or authors (if there were multiple authors) are also listed and separated by semicolons. We also have authors include their initials in parentheses after their names, as this makes it easier for clients to recognize who is who in the running resume and on invoices. Please see the report examples in Appendix B for more examples of how we name our reports' authors and recipients.

4. Include biographical information about the event or witness in the first paragraph.

Always include the subject's full first and last names, the location of the event and the physical description of the subject in the first paragraph. The biographical paragraph is meant to establish who and to what the report relates. If known, include the subject's Social Security number and date of birth, as well as a working phone number and other contact information for any additional information requests. Biographical data allows for quick identification of the document, proves that you were there and improves the chances that the evidence detailed in the report could later be verified or clarified. Because the information makes it easier for us to find, we can thereafter re-interview or subpoena the witness again at some time in the future. Also list any other additional contact information obtained during the interview in the first paragraph. For instance, if during the course of the interview, the subject provides you with his work phone number or the address of his sister where he will be staying, add that to the first paragraph. Again, the idea is that all contact information will be at the tip of your fingertips upon opening a document and you will not have to spend several minutes digging through multiple pages of a report to find a phone number. Templates should be designed to elicit this important information from the author. When the event transpired over two or more days, both dates should be clearly marked in this paragraph as well. In reports concerning telephone interviews, the called- or call-received-from phone number should be listed, absent a physical description.

Here are some examples of biographical paragraphs from two reports, the first for an in-person interview:

With reference to the above case, we interviewed Hal Kines, SSN unknown, DOB unknown, on December 12, 2009, by meeting with him at the ABC Property Management office located at 1814 Massachusetts Ave. NW, Washington, DC 20036. Kines is a residential maintenance supervisor for Acme Services, which performs maintenance at this and other ABC Property Management properties, which include several commercial and residential buildings in and around Washington, DC. Kines is described as a white male, approximately 5 feet, 11 inches tall, with a medium build and thinning, brown hair. He has a tattoo of an eagle on his outer left forearm. During the course of the interview, Kines said that he can best be reached at his home after 5 p.m., which is located at 2120 Connecticut Ave. NW, Washington, DC.

Now, here is another example for a telephonic interview:

With reference to the above, I interviewed Miles Archer, SSN unknown, DOB unknown, on July 9, 2008, by calling phone number 202-555-7412. Archer provided another number where he can be reached as 202-555-1283.

Background check memos will almost always contain the subject's Social Security number and date of birth to enhance credibility that the cases found belong to that specific subject, and not to someone with a similar name. This is exceedingly important when dealing with subjects with common names. However, you should not include the Social Security number or date of birth in the first paragraph if you are not certain that this information actually belongs to the subject of the investigation. The first paragraph is for information that is verified or reasonably certain. Since information obtained from an investigative database is never automatically verified, probable (but unverified) Social Security numbers and dates of birth should be included later in the report, with a qualifier that their authenticity is uncertain. Our firm differentiates information that is supplied before the initiation of the investigation from information discovered in database searches in this manner. In other words, to avoid confusion, information that is not confirmed or not actually observed by the investigator firsthand should not be included in the biographical paragraph; it should be included later in the report and must be properly qualified, or its source must be cited.

As an example, consider the following paragraph, which comes from the same report as the telephonic interview of Miles Archer above:

> Asked if he would be open to the possibility of meeting to sign a declaration, Archer told me that he would not and that we would need to subpoena him if he were to provide any more information.
>
> After Archer ended the telephone interview, I ran a database inquiry using his name and telephone number, and the search results indicated that an individual named Miles Archer, SSN 123-45-6789, DOB January 21, 1936, appears to reside at 1202 11th St., NW, Washington, DC 20010.

In this example, Archer's identifying information is not included in the biographical paragraph but much further down in the report, since its accuracy is unknown. We will further discuss citing sources or showing your work later in this chapter.

5. For witness-interview reports, also include an identification "disclaimer" paragraph.

After the first biographical paragraph comes what our firm calls the disclaimer paragraph. It is only used in witness-interview reports, where you should always include it immediately beneath the biographical paragraph. The disclaimer paragraph is intended to clearly indicate that you made clear the nature of the interview and that the subject knew who you were and agreed to speak to you regarding the matter under investigation. This is so vital because it is extremely common for witnesses and other subjects to later claim that private investigators misrepresented themselves as law enforcement or falsely claimed to work for the opposition in civil litigation. To counter these accusations, the way that you identify yourself to subjects should be the same in every case, so that you can always answer reliably what you told witnesses about your identity. The disclaimer need not be a verbatim statement of what you said to the witness, but it must at least indicate that you told the witness who you are and that they consented to the interview. If challenged later, this will lend additional credibility to your assertion that you properly identified yourself.

Our firm uses the following as its disclaimer paragraph:

After being advised of the identity of the interviewer and the nature of the investigation, John Dalmas agreed to be interviewed regarding the matter of Owen Taylor and ABC Bank and told me the following:

This language was largely copied from the format used in the FBI's FD-302 reports. If you showed the subject your identification card or provided them a business card, then that information should be included in this paragraph as well. Note that this paragraph separates the summary information from the substantive investigative report, which is why a colon is appropriate at the end of the paragraph.

6. Assume that the reader does not know anything about the case or how to investigate.

When considering the substance of an investigative report, the first fundamental principle is that the report should be written assuming that the reader does not know anything about the case or how to investigate. You must always prepare a report to be wholly understandable to someone not previously involved in the case who is picking up the investigative report for the first time. This is because cases often change hands, attorneys bring on new assistants and paralegals and new investigators may be brought on to a case. Your reports should therefore be prepared with an eye for allowing a new person to understand the facts and get brought up to speed quickly to participate in a case.

The investigator should avoid using investigative jargon in the report and should not write the report in the third person, except within the running resume. Jargon and ambiguous abbreviations and language only breed confusion, which can lead to misunderstandings regarding what the author is trying to convey. Remember that other readers of the report probably do not have the benefit of knowing the full backdrop of the investigation. They also probably do not have the benefit of your investigative experience. While the primary requester probably knows as much as you do, others on the legal team may not. Consider the following example:

> I asked whether or not Hoover's supervisor knew that Hoover was expecting his daughter to receive a job at ABC Bank following her graduation from college, and Wilson said that he did not know.

While the primary attorney working on the case may understand who Hoover's supervisor is, who Hoover's daughter is, and what position she wanted at the bank, this is hardly information that would be generally understandable to the fresh reader new to the case. To improve clarity and allow for easy digestion of investigative reports, any information not readily apparent should be included in the report. The above example should be rewritten as follows:

> I asked whether or not Hoover's supervisor, Richard Daley, knew that Hoover was expecting his daughter, Sarah, to receive a job at ABC Bank following her graduation from college, and Wilson said that he did not know.

In the new version, the reader can more readily determine the names of the people involved and their roles in a case. This allows for the most seamless possible transition for new participants joining an ongoing investigation.

On a related note, it is also important to properly identify acronyms and colloquial names. Our fast-paced, modern society is one that has become accustomed to shortened names and acronyms. For many workers firmly ensconced in a particular field, acronyms that have become a familiar mode of speaking can leave others, unfamiliar with the field, completely in the dark. Colloquial, familiar names are often adopted and utilized by certain groups more than their formal, proper-name counterparts. This is why it is always important to include a complete explanation of all unfamiliar acronyms and a full statement of proper names prior to utilizing a shortened, colloquial version. Consider the following example:

> I informed Herbert Hoover that the investigation concerned a violation of the EPPA.

Clearly, if you are working on a case regarding the Employee Polygraph Protection Act, then the attorneys you are working for on the case likely know what the acronym EPPA means. However, nobody else would likely know what you are referring to without the explanation. Therefore, unfamiliar acronyms should be written out and identified. The above sentence should be rewritten as:

> I informed Herbert Hoover that the investigation concerned a violation of the Employee Polygraph Protection Act ("EPPA").

Once you have identified the full term once, you can then use the acronym throughout the rest of the report. However, not all acronyms are treated the same. For acronyms that are commonplace in society, no explanation is needed. A good rule of thumb is whether or not a random person on the street would be able to tell you what the acronym stood for if asked. Therefore, while FBI and CIA are so common that they can be understood by virtually everyone, a reference to the JTTF (Joint Terrorism Task Force) would likely require an explanation. The acronyms and abbreviations in Appendix A are illustrative here. Generally, only the acronyms and abbreviations that are bolded may be used in reports without first defining the term.

The same will hold true for colloquial or familiar, shortened names. While many of these may be easily-identified by their shortened name, for professionalism purposes it is best to write out full proper names before using a colloquial version. This rule should especially be applied to those colloquial names that are not generally understood. Take the following examples:

> Asked whether or not Murray had entered the WitSec program, special agent Dwyer said that he was not at liberty to say.

> John Harris said that while living in New York City, he worked at the Met from 2001 to 2005.

When rewritten to include the full proper names, the report should look like this:

> Asked whether or not Murray had entered the Witness Security program ("WitSec"), special agent Dwyer said that he was not at liberty to say.

John Harris said that while living in New York City, he worked at the Metropolitan Museum of Art ("the Met") from 2001 to 2005.

The reason for these rules dovetails with the reason for including full explanations of facts in a case: a good investigator will document investigations that allow fresh eyes to be able to quickly read and comprehend a case, simply by reading his or her reports.

7. Do not draw conclusions or make assumptions.

It is critical that all reports describe the facts fairly and accurately and remain as objective as possible. Obviously, an investigator should never embellish facts, but it is also important that he or she be conscious of the tendency among novice investigators to either infer facts that were merely implied or to inadvertently imply facts or circumstances that are not clearly established by the evidence. One way to help ensure accuracy is to learn how to clearly recognize the distinction between an opinion that summarizes a set of facts and the facts themselves. You should never provide an opinion about the issue under investigation. For example, the statement that a witness lied is an opinion, and it would be inappropriate to make this statement in any investigative report. However, the specific, observed behaviors that inclined the investigator to believe that the subject was lying, for example, a latent response, might be legitimately included in a report. Consider the following example:

> I asked Cairo whether he stole the money. After a significant pause, when the subject was observed putting his hand over his mouth, he responded, "I did not steal that money."

In this example, we are not stating that Cairo lied in his response to this question, but we are noting significant behaviors that we observed in response to this question that could raise suspicion as to its veracity.

To provide another example, during an interview, an investigator must also carefully differentiate facts from the opinions of others as well. In other words, you must distinguish between those facts that a witness personally knows from the witness's opinions disguised as facts. Often these opinions are based on nothing more than hearsay.

By asking questions during the interview that establish a witness's basis of opinion, often it is possible to identify the observable facts that led the witness to that opinion. For example, if a witness describes a person as "angry"–clearly an opinion–you might then ask him to describe the behaviors that led him to his belief that the person was angry. This basis of belief may be built upon legitimate, observable facts, such as a subject having a raised voice or being "red-faced." This descriptive information should be included in the report to establish why the witness thought the subject was angry. In the above example, without the establishment of the basis of belief, the fact that the witness merely believed the subject was angry is otherwise an unsubstantiated opinion.

8. Show your work.

Clients give a lot of credence to our reports, and they take the things that we write in our reports at face value. This is why it is so critical to always properly qualify your findings and cite your sources. In other words, you should always state how you know what you know and admit to the limitations of your knowledge. For example, unless you are certain about a subject's residency, the source of this information should be attributed to "credit header information" (when gleaned from investigative databases). This is important, as the only way to verify residency with absolute certainty is to actually witness the subject living at the address. Since this is unlikely to happen, you should always write what you observed or specifically how it was learned. Investigative databases really only show that someone has had a *connection* to a given address.

Here is an example that demonstrates one way to show your work:

> Murdoch told me that she learned from Sam LNU that Brody is presently residing in Mississippi. Through an investigative database search, I was able to locate a possib address for Brody in Biloxie.

On a related note, always include some of the information that was provided at the initiation of the investigation that leads you to conclude that the subject or subjects discussed in the interview are the correct people. As you already know, do not include the subject's Social Security number or date of birth in the biographical paragraph unless they were known at the beginning of the investigation or unless you are certain they belong to the subject. When searching for locations of witnesses, it is important to include whatever additional information led you to believe that the person is residing at that location. This can also help later to determine a timeline for when that witness may have lived at that location if he or she later cannot be found there. In other words, always show your work and cite it to attachments (e.g., court records) when appropriate. However, never send database printouts as attachments. Investigative databases—as their disclaimers indicate—are for informational purposes only, and they must never be confused with the reality that we can observe with our own eyes. In fact, the issue of residency should always be confirmed with a second source (preferably government or utility, such as county property records or public telephone listings) before it is ever put into an investigative report.

An additional way of showing your work comes from post-interview research. Often, as investigators, we are confronted with statements of fact or, more often, with unsure statements, that induce us to conduct additional research. When a witness states that he was a starting forward on the University of Maryland's men's basketball team for three years and we are unsure as to the statement's veracity, a cursory Internet search could confirm whether or not this is true. Or, where a witness tells us that he knows of another witness who works at a "bar on Magazine and Napoleon Streets," but could not recall the name of the bar, you should conduct research to try and determine to what bar he is referring. This practice is imperative for providing your clients with complete, accurate and informative investigative reports and sets you apart from other investigators who may simply report what is said and nothing more. Clients prefer investigators who take the initiative, and conducting post-interview research to clarify or verify facts is one of those small steps that can have a major impact. A good way of delineating between post-interview research and witness statements is to include the additional information as a footnote. In the latter example, the footnote could read:

> Upon further investigation using Google Street View, I was able to determine that a bar called Club Ms. Mae's, located at 4336 Magazine Street, New Orleans, LA, is the only bar on the corner of Magazine and Napoleon Streets.

This practice will not only help your clients to better understand the facts of their cases, but also to provide further documentation of leads in an ongoing investigation.

9. Address any unanswered questions up front.

It is also important to make sure that the report answers all questions that a reader could have about its contents. It is all too common for clients to respond to reports with a question such as, "Did you ask the witness *this* question?" Or, "Did you search for records in *this* location?" You should foresee these questions and include the answer in the report. In interview reports, you should include each question asked and the subject's response. Here is a sample from one of our reports:

> I asked Dodd about Knapp's whereabouts, and he told me that he does not know. Asked about the last time that he saw Knapp, he said that he last saw her in 2007, at a family barbeque. I asked Dodd if he has any information about where Knapp could be staying, and he said that he heard that she was somewhere in Mississippi—but that he is unsure if this is true. Asked where he heard this from, Dodd said that he cannot remember.

In the above example, there should be little question that Dodd is not going to be more helpful in helping our investigator find Knapp, because there were no questions left unanswered.

For background check reports, you should state why information not included in the report—but that would be reasonably expected to be included in the report—was unavailable. For example, perhaps the court records in a particular jurisdiction were only available for 10 years, but a known criminal conviction occurred 11 years ago. In such an instance, include a statement about the scope of the search, so that the obvious question is answered before the client can think to ask it.

Consider the following example:

> I ran a criminal records search on Knapp in Mississippi and Virginia, which are reportedly the only two states where she has

resided. I was unable to find any information about her 1992 arrest for solicitation in Arlington County, Virginia, because the state's district courts destroy records of misdemeanors after 10 years.

This paragraph answers the obvious question of why a known arrest is not included in the report: the record was unavailable. You should always foresee these types of questions and make sure that you answer them before the client can even think to ask.

10. Have the report reviewed and edited by a third-party prior to sending it to the client.

Finally, all reports should be reviewed for any spelling mistakes, punctuation errors or unclear wording by a second investigator or by an editor employed by the investigative firm for that purpose. The importance of this review cannot be overstated. Authors are conditioned to miss many of their mistakes in their own writing, even if they read the same document over several times. Your mind too often cannot separate what it expects to read from what is actually written on the page. A fresh set of eyes is all that it takes to catch the majority of these credibility-destroying errors. At our firm, we contract to an outside editor who remains on call to review our reports as needed. At other firms—and at ours when our editor is unavailable—the review is typically done by the case's lead investigator or its case manager. However, the review can theoretically be done by anyone, even another investigator or an administrative employee.

It is the job of the reviewer to catch and fix every single error on the report, be it unclear wording or formatting that is inconsistent with the company's uniform style guidelines. The names of each reviewer should be included in the report on the footer, and all changes made to the report should be carefully tracked. This level of transparency is so vital because the opposition may later claim that the original report was substantially altered, calling into question the evidence as detailed in the report. After the report has been reviewed and edited, the reviewer should save the marked document to an appropriate subfolder and any changes that are not merely spelling, grammar or clarifying corrections must be approved by the report's author. Anything that may be unclear and not immediately correctable by the reviewer should be referred to the writer of the report for clarification. Reviewers should never change anything substantive in quotations without first clearing the change with the report's author.

Once the report has been reviewed and finalized, the draft should be archived as a digital file, and the final version should then be converted to an Adobe Acrobat .pdf file or a similarly immutable format and placed in the appropriate subfolder for that case. That final file should then be forwarded to the investigator who composed it or to the case manager for delivery to the client. In other words, the report should ideally come from the investigator who prepared it. If, for whatever reason, an assigning investigator cannot deliver the final reviewed report to the client (e.g., because he or she is out in the field at the time that it was reviewed), the investigator can request that the reviewer send the final report directly to the appropriate parties, as listed in the report heading. Our firm sends out all of our reports to clients using the TrackOps system. This is done by creating a running resume update and attaching the report to the update. There is then a drop-down menu that allows us to highlight the appropriate recipients (which are also named in the report heading). The important part is that the client does not see the draft or necessarily know what went into the review process; they only see a flawlessly written report.

Chapter 7

STATEMENTS

Another important facet of documenting an investigation is obtaining sworn affidavits, declarations and verbatim statements from witnesses that can later be used in court by attorneys to refresh witnesses' recollections or to impeach (call into question) their testimony. The principal difference between affidavits and declarations is that an affidavit must be signed and sworn to before a notary public, while declarations do not require a notary seal. Investigators may find it useful to also become licensed notaries in the jurisdictions where they routinely work in order to more easily obtain affidavits. However, state and federal law generally allow declarations into evidence in most instances. The procedures for obtaining sworn declarations are fundamentally the same as for obtaining affidavits, so we will essentially treat them the same in this book.

What differentiates a statement from a declaration or an affidavit essentially boils down to its format. What investigators are typically referring to when they say "statement" is a verbatim statement taken from a witness immediately following an interview. In contrast, declarations and affidavits are obtained after reviewing the investigative report concerning an interview and later asking the witness to sign an abbreviated statement, called a declaration or an affidavit, which only addresses the specific, relevant evidence in the case. *From a strictly legal standpoint, all affidavits and declarations are types of statements, and what we are referring to here as a verbatim statement could even be considered an affidavit or a declaration, depending on the language used in the document. The distinctions that we are making in this chapter relate to the form that the document takes, not its distinct legal classification.

To reiterate one of the Five Principles of Investigative Documentation, the choice of which type of statement to use will depend generally upon the perceived degree of cooperation of the witness, the relevance of the witness to the case, the content of the witness's likely testimony, and the type and even applicable jurisdiction of the case. Although somewhat counterintuitive, the general rule is that the more cooperative and helpful a witness, the less you should seek to lock the witness into his or her account. In this situation, a declaration or an affidavit is the most appropriate vehicle to preserve the witness's testimony. Conversely, the less cooperative or more harmful a witness, the more you will want to lock the witness into his or her account at the time the statement is made, making a verbatim statement more ideal—because the more detail an uncooperative witness provides, the more opportunity there is for possible impeachment during trial. The decision not to lock helpful witnesses into detailed and potentially damaging testimony is critical, since statements—unlike all of the other forms of documentation discussed in this book—are usually discoverable by the opposition.

1. Take sworn verbatim statements from hostile or unhelpful witnesses

Verbatim statements are taken immediately after the conclusion of an interview, when the witness is still present and before the investigator prepares a report. Statements may be written by the witness or dictated by the witness and written by the investigator. The method is generally a matter of personal preference and practicality. For dictated statements, you inform the witness that you want to write down a verbatim account of the events to ensure accuracy and then ask the witness to reiterate what he or she said during the interview, starting from the beginning. You should actually avoid using the word "statement," however, which sounds too legalistic, and you should never explicitly ask someone whether they will agree or consent to provide a statement. The witness will have a choice when it comes to actually signing the document. At that point in the process, the witness has much more invested in the document, making it more likely that he or she will sign it.

Instead of asking whether the witness consents to providing a statement, simply state the need to get the facts straight, take out a clean notepad and ask the witness to start again from the beginning. You should write down what the witness says word-for-word, being sure to skip lines on the notepad to provide space for any corrections, until the witness relays the entire event again in one continuous narrative. While it is acceptable to ask the witness questions during this monologue or to ask the witness to slow down or clarify a particular area, the statement should reflect the event entirely in the witness's own words. Sometimes, however, an investigator will choose to include questions within the statement, as in the following example:

Q: What did you do after you saw the gun?
A: Well, when I saw the gun I was just, like, scared, you know, and I started running down the street.

After writing out the complete statement by hand, you should add language substantially similar to the below example on the header and footer of the document. Sometimes, investigators use prepared statement forms that already contain this language. A sample of a statement template is included in Appendix D of this book, along with an example of what a completed statement should look like. When forms are not used, however, it is best to begin with the statement before writing the header, skipping several lines on the top of the first page of the statement to allow enough space for the header after completion of the statement. At the beginning of the statement, write:

This is the statement of Victor Trevor, DOB July 4, 1901, SSN 123-45-6789, 3500 13th St., NW, Washington, DC 20010, given to Sam Spade, an investigator working for attorney Richard Nixon. Mr. Nixon represents Sam Merton in the case of Sam Merton v. City Corporation, Ltd. in the Superior Court of the District of Columbia. This statement was taken at 2015 Connecticut Ave., NW, Washington, DC 20006 on November 11, 2007, at approximately 12:31 p.m.

It is okay if the witness refuses to provide his or her Social Security number or date of birth. The investigator should simply collect whatever information the witness will provide. At the footer, following the substantive body of the statement he or she should insert the following language:

I have read and have had read to me this [number of pages] page statement [and attached document, diagram, or photograph, if applicable]. I have had an opportunity to make any corrections, deletions, and/or additions to this statement. I solemnly affirm under penalty of perjury that this statement is true, correct and complete.

Although this language is not necessarily required to make the statement useful for purposes of impeachment, the sworn oath and signature gives the document an appearance of authority in the eyes of a jury and makes it a more effective source of impeachment.

After completing a verbatim statement and writing the above language at the header and footer of the statement, you should position the document such that both you and the witness can read it simultaneously. You should then—pointing at every word with the tip of a pen or a similar instrument—read the entire statement to the witness as the witness reads along silently. You should ask the witness if he or she can read the handwriting to establish literacy, all the while paying special attention to such factors as whether the witness is wearing glasses and whether his or her eyes are moving in conjunction with the direction of the pen.

With every necessary change, you should draw a single line through the verbiage that must be excised—never completely scratch out a word or sentence—and ask the witness to initial the changes. Additions should be added within the skipped lines. This is the reason why double-spacing is so important. The witness should then initial both in the front and in the back of any additions. Upon the completion of each page of the statement that reads exactly as what the witness said and where the witness has initialed at the start and end of each and every addition and deletion, you should ask the witness to sign and date the page. You should then inconspicuously take that page and place it outside of the witness's reach, such as in a briefcase. Otherwise, the witness may try to take it back. In the event that the witness changes his or her mind about signing a statement in the middle of the process, the completed pages retained by the investigator may still be useful. The final statement may be significantly marked up with edits and initials, but this is okay, because it shows that the statement was given voluntarily and it proves that the witness had ample opportunity to make changes. The statement is now represents a detailed account of the witness's likely testimony that can be extremely powerful impeachment evidence if the witness decides to change his or her story later on.

For statements written by the witness or typed out on the spot, the process is substantially similar, although the investigator necessarily sacrifices some control in the former and spontaneity in the latter. For example, if the witness is tasked with writing his or her own statement, it may be difficult for you to assure that the witness follows the necessary format and stays on topic. With typed statements, it may be impractical or awkward to bring a laptop and a printer to the field during an interview. Otherwise, you should obtain these statements exactly the same as with other verbatim statements. It is still necessary to include the legal necessities, to review the entire completed statement with the witness word for word, and to allow the witness to make corrections.

After taking a verbatim statement, prepare an investigative report summarizing the salient portions of the interview (see Chapter 6).

2. Draft declarations or affidavits for friendly witnesses.

In contrast to verbatim statements, declarations and affidavits are typically obtained sometime after the interview and after the completion of the interview report. Because declarations and affidavits are only distinguished by whether they are notarized or not, we will hereafter refer to them collectively as declarations. The goal of a declaration is not exclusively for the purposes of impeachment; rather, it also preserves helpful testimony in its most pristine form. Usually, a declaration in the form of an affidavit is admissible as stand-alone testimonial evidence for example to support or oppose a motion for summary judgment in a civil case.

Whenever concluding an interview where no verbatim statement was taken, you should determine at the conclusion of the interview if the witness is "open to the possibility" of signing a declaration. This language is important, because most people will be open to the possibility of something, even if they ultimately decide against it. By asking the question in this manner, it allows you to leave your foot in the door to later approach the witness about giving a declaration. You should then prepare an interview report and a draft declaration. When preparing for secondary meetings with witnesses to obtain declarations, you should write as much of the witness's declaration as possible in advance of the meeting. This will save time and make the process smoother, allowing you to fill in the blanks and supplement the declaration with new information. You can then anticipate what the witness will say, based upon the earlier interview. While it is ideal to have the same investigator return to obtain the signed declaration, it is not a strict requirement. In the event that a second investigator is conducting the follow-up interview, he or she will be guided by the information contained in your investigative report and even other, third-party accounts, such as those of the client or other witnesses. When preparing draft declarations, it is acceptable to fill in the gaps with what you expect to be true, based upon other evidence gathered during the investigation. In the event that the witness has no firsthand knowledge of the confusing information in the draft, it can easily be deleted. For declarations and affidavits, you should draft the document in a manner that is ideal from the standpoint of the case's hypothesis, provided that it is consistent with what the witness previously said and with the other known facts of the case.

All declarations and affidavits essentially follow the same format:

My name is Victor Trevor. I am over eighteen (18) years of age, competent to testify, and I make this affidavit having personal knowledge of the following facts:

1. [Substance in concise language]

2. [Substance in concise language, etc.]

I solemnly affirm, under penalty of perjury, that the contents of the foregoing affidavit are true and correct to the best of my knowledge, information and belief.

_____   _____
Victor Trevor   Date

A sample of a completed declaration is included in Appendix D.

For each substantive numbered point, you should sum up the facts of the case in succinct, chronological paragraphs, written in the first person from the standpoint of the witness, listing the date, exact setting, names of the actors, the tone and scenario in as much detail as possible. You may also attach exhibits referenced in the body of the declaration. If the witness insists on being "fair" to a particular subject by adding unnecessary information, you may add normally inadmissible and generalized comments so as to give the good with the bad. Consider the following example for a racial discrimination case:

13. Although I thought Mr. Williams was an excellent manager, he frequently referred to Asian-American employees as "those gooks."

Mr. Williams may or may not have been a good manager, but he still frequently used a racial slur to refer to his Asian-American employees. Notice that in the above example, the real word is used for the offensive racial slur, instead of a paraphrase or abbreviation. For declarations, as opposed to verbatim statements, what does not help the case may actually hurt it (because the witness is altogether helpful to the case), so it is important to avoid admissible information that does not support the hypothesis. You should be extra careful with qualifiers and not put the witness in a position where he or she will be impeached by absolutes. As with verbatim statements, you should always be sure to include the page number and date on the footer of every page of the document and to have the witness initial and date every page.

It is essential that you know the law and how to incorporate it wherever possible, keeping at the forefront what you are trying to prove in the case and how it will be introduced into evidence. For example, you should never merely summarize an important statement when it is possible to use quotation marks, which will increase the likelihood that the statement will be admissible. You should also draft the declaration with hearsay exceptions in mind. Recalling that one hearsay exception is an excited utterance, consider the below example.

16. In a fit of excitement Mrs. Washington uttered, "Get your hands off of me!"

Now that you have a draft declaration, you are ready to meet with the witness again to get the declaration signed. Below are the procedures that our firm's investigators use to increase the odds of getting solid declarations in our cases.

3. Pick an advantageous location.

It is always best to conduct interviews, including follow-up interviews, at the investigative firm's office. However because of considerations concerning the witness's convenience, it is sometimes necessary to meet in a public place near the witness's home or work. As the investigator, you should take the initiative to pick a location that is advantageous. The location must be relatively quiet and comfortable. Restaurants are excellent meeting points for declarations, and the booths of restaurants are best, as there is a lot of surface area and privacy. During this second interview to obtain a declaration, you should bring a laptop computer, a portable, battery-powered printer and all necessary cables. Remember to have a full charge on all batteries, as there may be no power source at the location. Completing a declaration may take well over an hour. It is also important to consider extra paper and extra ink cartridges. Upon entering the restaurant (or whichever location you choose), you should determine if there are any electrical outlets nearby. Even the most advanced and fully charged laptop batteries only last a few hours. As some declaration meetings have been known to last more than four hours, it is important to be prepared.

4. Avoid creating drafts.

During the meeting, you should avoid printing or saving drafts, as they may be discoverable, and losing or destroying them could lead to a spoliation allegation (a claim that evidence was destroyed, often resulting in sanctions by the court, including dismissal of the case). In other words, you should make all changes digitally and only print the document when it is perfect. Sometimes, however, drafts are unavoidable, because witnesses may want to make changes at the last minute. You may not have perfect knowledge of the case, but the witness probably will not know this, so you should talk with confidence and listen carefully to the witness, continually incorporating his or her answers into the declaration. A witness will often disclose a great deal of information when he or she thinks you already know what happened. It is generally acceptable at this stage to tell the witness what other witnesses have said and to ask the witness to confirm whether he or she also witnessed the same. You must take ample time to proofread the final draft for any grammatical, spelling or other mistakes, as the declaration is probably discoverable once it is printed and reviewed by the witness. When ready to print, read the declaration aloud to the witness and ask him or her to confirm that it is entirely correct before printing it out, thereby avoiding drafts and committing him or her to the story.

5. Take the best that you can get under the circumstances.

In the event that the witness refuses to sign the final declaration (or verbatim statement, for that matter), you should never agree to give the witness a draft to sign and return at a later date. If the witness will not sign it at that time and you do not believe the witness will sign it later, leaving the draft document with the witness will allow it to fall into the hands of the opposition. One alternative for a witness in a criminal defense investigation who refuses to sign a statement is to offer to allow them to initial every page and sign the document on a line that states, "Refused to Sign." While this is not preferable over a signed statement, it nonetheless provides additional proof that you were actually present and indeed interviewed the witness, in case you later are called as an impeachment witness. Similarly, you should avoid e-mailing drafts or final versions to a witness, as the document, drafts and even metadata will likely end up in the opponent's hands. Metadata is data embedded in most digital files that typically includes information such as when the file was created and altered. As with verbatim statements, once the document is signed, you should immediately place it in your bag or otherwise out of the witness's reach. If the document is left on the table, the witness may ask for it back.

It is sometimes necessary to obtain declarations from witnesses who are not local and can only be spoken to on the phone. You should determine the likelihood that the witness will return a signed declaration of his or her own accord, based upon the degree of cooperation that a witness exhibited during the interview. It is always better to hire a local investigator to personally deliver the declaration to the witness for signature, and this advice should be relayed to the client. In the event the client does not want to shoulder the extra cost of hiring an outside operative, you should call the witness with the draft declaration open on your computer screen. You should remind the witness that he or she expressed "openness" to signing a declaration and ask the witness if he or she has a few minutes to go over a draft. If he or she claims not to have time, reschedule for another time. The key is to get a time and date scheduled. If the witness does have a few minutes, review the entire declaration with him or her from top to bottom and make edits during the call, trying to keep the language in the declaration as close to what is in the draft as possible. If you decide to hire an outside investigator to deliver the declaration, you should advise the witness that someone will be in touch with him or her within the next few days to arrange to deliver the document for signature.

If you decide not to hire an investigator, you should ask the witness for his or her e-mail address and send an e-mail substantially similar to the below example, with the declaration as a .pdf or similar immutable document attached:

Dear Mr. Wheeler:

With reference to our conversation a few minutes ago, please find attached the declaration that we produced. Once you have had a chance to review this again, please forward a signed copy to me by fax at the fax number below or by scanned attachment to e-mail, and mail the original to my office at the address below. Feel free to make any necessary minor changes, but please call me first if you need to change any of the substantive language. You can make minor changes by putting a single line through any words that you would like to remove and writing any words that you would like to add in the spaces between the lines, making sure to initial both the start and end of each alteration.

Let me know if you have any questions or need more information. Thanks for your help!

[Add e-mail signature here.]

See Chapter 2 for more information regarding how to and how not to communicate with witnesses using e-mail.

If you need to hire an outside investigator, do so now, after the witness has already agreed to the language in the declaration. Simply send a digital copy of the declaration to the outside investigator with the witness's contact information and clear instructions to obtain the signature. Once the outside investigator has obtained the signed declaration, he or she should fax or e-mail *and* mail a copy to you directly. If you do not receive the e-mailed or faxed affidavit within a couple days, you should contact the witness (or the outside investigator should, as applicable) to politely remind them to send the declaration as soon as possible. You should do the same thing if you do not receive the mailed original within a couple weeks. The declaration should be mailed to your office, so that the investigative firm, and not the client (e.g., the law firm), can remain responsible for ensuring its completion. Finally, you should copy and then forward the original, executed declaration to the client as soon as it is received.

Once you have statements from everyone in the case, you will probably just wait until the case goes to trial or settles. We will now discuss what we do with the documents that we generate during our investigations.

Chapter 8

DOCUMENT RETENTION

Most of our cases involve working for attorneys who typically have their own requirements for maintaining records. These requirements vary by state, but they typically require lawyers to keep records for anywhere from five to 10 years. While these rules do not necessarily apply to investigators, maintaining records is an important sound business practice for us as well. Not all of our records are automatically sent to our clients, including our law-firm clients. There are some documents, like notes, that are almost never sent to clients. There are other documents, like running resumes, that we may opt to send to our clients but that we are not required to send to them. In litigation, however, we are two steps removed from the litigant, who is our client's client. When our client (the law firm) separates from its client, this often puts investigators in an awkward position. Certainly we stop working on the case, if or until we are retained to work on the case by the next law firm that represents the litigant. But what do we do with all the records of our investigation? Who owns these records? And what responsibility do investigators have to maintain copies? The litigant or the new attorneys may need to review our documents, including our notes and running resumes, at some later time. Although we may not have a specific legal obligation to help people who we are no longer working for, we argue here that investigators have an ethical obligation to maintain their records for a reasonable period of time, such that the records may be available to whoever works on a case after us. This obligation is amplified in criminal defense investigations, where new evidence or favorable appeals give defendants another shot at maintaining their innocence—sometimes years later and—

the fruits of our investigation once again become integral to a person's freedom. Keep in mind as well that whoever follows in our footsteps may choose to subpoena us for this information as well, which is all the more reason why having a stated document retention and destruction policy is so prudent.

One way to make sure that all documents are maintained for an appropriate amount of time is to transfer all of the investigative firm's documentations, including notes, the running resumes and any work-product that was not already submitted as an attachment on a report, to the law firm at the conclusion of the case. Let the lawyers deal with the issue of document retention. If this is your policy, then that is all that you need to do, and you can skip reading the rest of this chapter.

Many investigative firms, however, do not like to turn over their notes unless it is required. Notes show our work when it is at its most raw, with misspellings and allusions to promising leads that never materialized. There is a good reason why criminal defense attorneys scour through the police officers' notes that they receive in discovery. Taken out of context, even well-prepared notes can sometimes make even the best investigator appear incompetent. The reason this does not matter during an open case is that investigators confronted with their notes on the stand can easily explain them. What makes many of us uncomfortable is handing over notes without the opportunity to explain them.

For firms that choose not to automatically turn over their notes to clients, I recommend maintaining most notes and all other records for a period of at least five years. Cases have a way of resurfacing several years after it was assumed that they were completed. It is not uncommon for an investigator working with a different attorney to contact you about a case years later, long after the law firm that originally hired you withdrew from the case. In these instances, it is very helpful to have access to your records. *What follows in the rest of this chapter is our firm's policy regarding document retention and destruction. It should be noted that the following retention policy is provided only as an example and suggestions. All investigators should discuss retention with their attorney–clients and tailor their own policies to fit with the statutes of limitations in their applicable jurisdiction.

DOCUMENT RETENTION

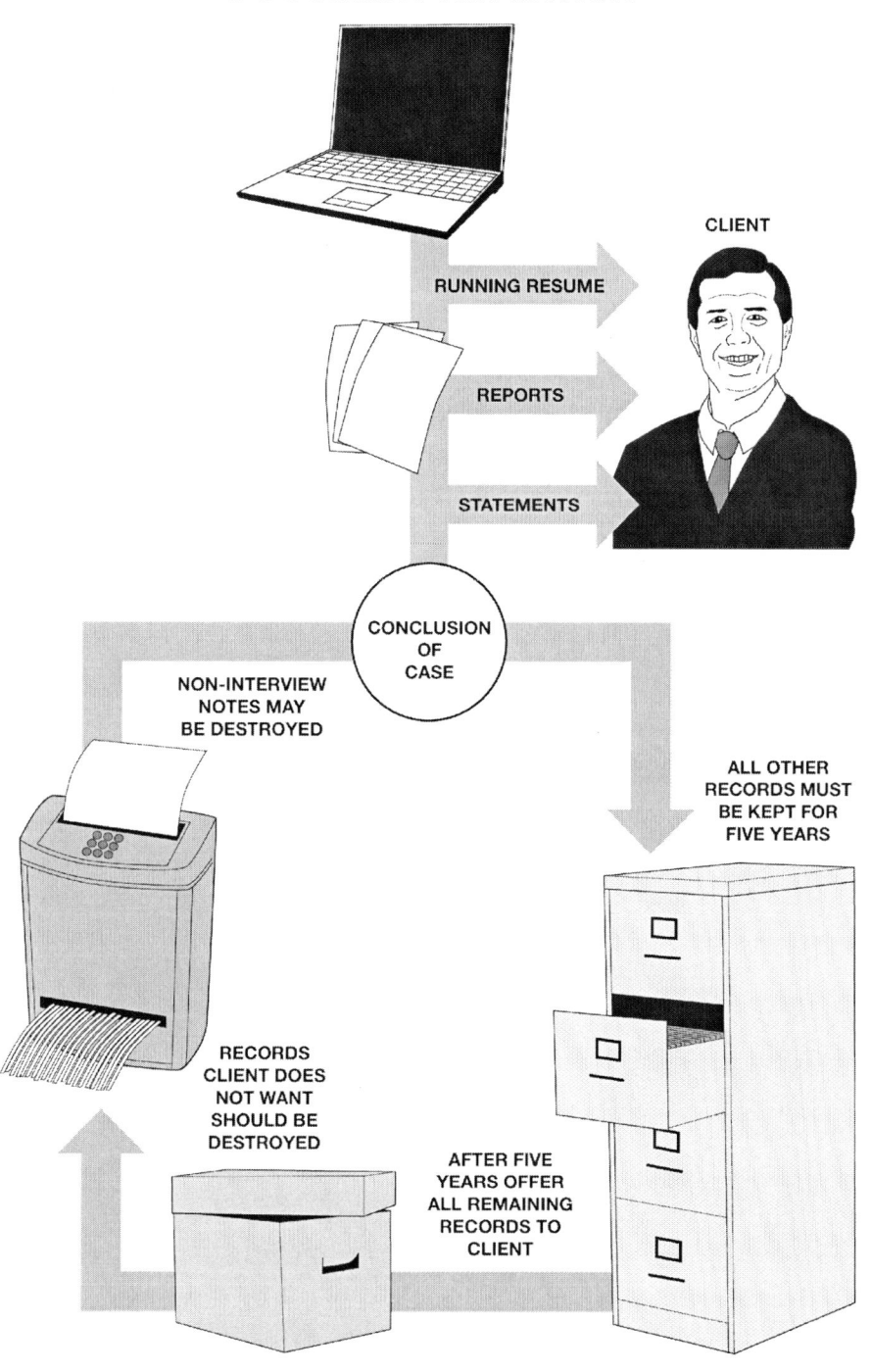

CLIENT

RUNNING RESUME

REPORTS

STATEMENTS

CONCLUSION OF CASE

NON-INTERVIEW NOTES MAY BE DESTROYED

ALL OTHER RECORDS MUST BE KEPT FOR FIVE YEARS

RECORDS CLIENT DOES NOT WANT SHOULD BE DESTROYED

AFTER FIVE YEARS OFFER ALL REMAINING RECORDS TO CLIENT

1. Give reports, statements and relevant third-party records to clients immediately.

If all investigators produced were reports, statements and vital third-party records (e.g., court records), then the task of document retention would be very easy, as these documents are sent to clients immediately upon completion anyway, creating no objective need for the investigative firm to retain them. Reports, original statements and third-party records belong to our clients, and that is who is primarily responsible for maintaining them. This is not to argue that we should not also keep these documents ourselves—we should always keep copies of everything we hand to clients—but it is to say that our policies are based mostly on the need to do something with the documents that we do *not* give to our clients. These records include working notes, e-mails and third-party records that were deemed to be irrelevant to the investigation.

Third-party records include any documentary evidence obtained from people who are not parties in the litigation. These records include, for example, court jackets, records subpoenaed from companies and documents obtained through the Freedom of Information Act. For example, pretend that, while trying to find an individual, you should decide to order her ex-husband's criminal record to see if there are any domestic violence cases that might indicate her whereabouts. When you receive the records, you learn that all of his convictions concern drugs and that there is nothing relevant in them that will help lead you to your subject. The ex-husband otherwise has nothing to do with your case. In this example, these records do not need to be turned over to the client, but they should be maintained to show that the lead was followed but did not pan out. We will discuss what to do with records that we keep but do not send to clients later in this chapter.

At our firm, final reports are sent to clients using our case management system. They are sent to clients as attachments to our running resume updates. Statements are scanned and sent in the same manner, and then the originals are either sent via FedEx or they are hand-delivered to the client. Original, third-party records that are relevant to the investigation are sent directly to the client without necessarily being copied or scanned, unless we may need to access them later in the investigation. In most instances, third-party records are sent as attachments to our reports. The reason we do not always maintain copies of these records is that we can normally obtain the third-party records again if we need them, so there is no compelling need to take up storage space by keeping another copy.

To illustrate by way of another example, say that a client asks us to do a background check on a client and to obtain certified copies of all convictions. Our investigator does the background check, obtains the court records, writes the report and then sends the report, along with scanned versions of the court documents, to the client. The original, certified records are then hand-delivered to the client. Our firm would likely not keep the original hard-copies of the court records. Everything that is of value is already in the report and its attachments, which are stored on our server.

2. Create a simple filing system for storing information during an ongoing investigation.

The best investigators distinguish themselves from others by being responsible with all information received during the course of an investigation. This is why, while investigating an open case, investigators must utilize a consistent, easy-to-use system for organizing interview and other notes, documents, reports, photographs and other pertinent information. One easy way to do this is to keep a master accordion file for each case, organized by the client or client-litigant. Within that file should be individual folders for different subcategories of information, such as folders for individual witnesses (including interviews and background/location data), surveillance locations and relevant court documents. Once you reach a witness, you should put your completed notes in its respective subfolder until it is time to write a report. Once complete, the investigative reports go into that folder as well, along with the returned interview notes. While some people have a different style, we suggest keeping interview notes and reports alongside any pertinent contact information, background check documents or database (skip trace) searches in witness-specific folders.

While it may seem tedious, maintaining a consistent file folder system for all your cases will help you to responsibly organize a case, allow for lightning-fast retrieval of information and safeguard against devastating losses of notes, data and other documents.

3. Establish a routine policy for document retention and communicate this with clients.

The most important thing about a document retention policy is its predictability. This is why establishing a written, formal document retention policy that fits your organization's specific needs is integral for any private investigation firm. Again, the period of time that attorneys have to keep their records varies somewhat, and there are no clearly established guidelines regarding the appropriate amount of time that investigators should maintain their firm's investigative records. If you turn over everything, including notes, to the law firm that you are working for, then theoretically you could destroy all of your copies immediately, but we do not know any investigative firm that does that. What many firms do is maintain their records indefinitely until they run out of room, and then they scramble for a solution. Storing records requires space–physical and digital space–and a system for cataloging and retrieving these files. Off-site storage costs money in storage costs and work hours. A document retention policy, therefore, has to balance the benefits of keeping the records with the hassle of managing an ever-burgeoning file system filled with thousands of files, many of which we will never need. In our view, five years from the conclusion of a case is a sufficient amount of time, a nice round number and a time period long enough to satisfy most legal requirements. Once you have decided on the appropriate time for your firm, draft up the policy in the form of an internal memo, bring it to the attention of all of your investigators and keep it on file at your office.

As with your investigators, clients too should be aware of your document retention policy, and they should receive a copy of the policy at the outset of your services. This is even more important for large, corporate clients who may become the subject of litigation and as such, must have strict document-retention policies of their own. While it is not advisable to let each client individually dictate his or her own preferences for the retention of their documents, you should have a discussion about this policy with any clients who may be the frequent subject of litigation–if for nothing more than to communicate the policy clearly. If the client is uncomfortable with your document retention policy, simply allow them to retrieve all of the files related to their case immediately upon the closing of the case. This shifts the burden of retention onto the client and frees up additional space for other clients' storage.

4. At the conclusion of a case, move all files to inactive status.

When a case is closed it is time to prepare your active files for inactive storage and toll your policy's clock for document retention. One way to do this is by moving the master file and any additional information in a given case, to file cabinets or some other kind of physical storage system. A good way to keep track of the cases is to arrange them by the year in which they went inactive. Therefore, you can easily group together closed cases and provide for orderly disposal of the folders at the conclusion of your stated retention policy. Inactive folders can be demarcated in a number of different ways: through colored stickers distinguishing the year when a case was moved to inactive, through distinct drawers in a file cabinet for certain years or simply by writing the year and the case name across the top of the folder and placing it into a box for storage.

At this point is also the time to destroy any unwanted information that does not apply to the retention policy. For example, notes not involving interviews can generally be destroyed. These notes include notes taken during meetings with the client; sticky notes Word documents used to jot down information during research; as well as any notes and even audio files used during surveillance. The reason why it is okay to destroy these records is that everything they contain deemed to be potentially meaningful will be documented in the running resume and reports anyway. E-mails with witnesses and notes concerning interviews, however, likely *do* contain information not contained in the running resume, and keeping them may be necessary to introduce a report into evidence in the event that the case is reactivated and you need to impeach the person you interviewed. For other types of working notes, transfer their content throughout the investigation onto the running resume and your reports (if applicable), and then shred or delete them when you move the case to inactive status.

5. Execute your policy after the retention period has been concluded.

Just because we have a policy that states we keep our records for five years does not necessarily mean that we automatically destroy everything at that time. At least once a year, you should review the files in storage and find those that have surpassed your retention period. You should then send an e-mail to your client notifying them that you are going to destroy the file, and give them 30 days to let you know whether they want it or not. If they inform you that they want the file, you should forward them the witness e-mails and the entire paper file, which primarily contain our interview notes, un-served subpoenas and any other items that were deemed irrelevant when the case was still active. Recall that they already have the other material, including all of the reports, statements and relevant third-party documents. When you are working for law firms, it is important to give them the option to take the records off your hands before they are irrevocably destroyed. Their document retention requirements may be more stringent than yours. Again, if you hand over everything at the conclusion of the case and all relevant information is recorded in the running resume, then there is arguably no reason for keeping any records at all. What we have found though is that having our own policies allows us to maintain our own interview notes while still retaining the documents for a reasonable period of time. After five years, many clients do not want the file anyway. If we do not get a response from the client, we destroy the documents.

It can be helpful to keep a spreadsheet showing when the client 30-day letter was sent; what, if anything, was sent to the client and the date; and the date that the file was destroyed. We also advocate maintaining a copy of the running resume indefinitely, however, as its format means that it does not require much space. It provides a fairly detailed record of everything that was done in a case that can be useful much later for training or other purposes. Also, because we use a computer program to send our reports and statements, these documents will be stored indefinitely. You can do this as well by keeping original electronic versions of your reports in specific folders on your company's server or on a removable hard drive. When it comes time to destroy records, paper files and notes go into a cross-cut shredder, and unwanted electronic version reports and other records are deleted to make space for new cases. We recommend using a software system like PGP (which stands for "Pretty Good Privacy") that will securely wipe away the file, in case it contains any confidential data. Although you may have stopped working on the case five years earlier, it is only now that your responsibility to maintain the records for that case officially ends.

6. Be mindful of special ethical concerns in retaining criminal defense records.

It is an extremely unfortunate circumstance when we hear of an innocent man or woman who was sent to prison for several years, sometimes decades, only to be released when new evidence or DNA is discovered, proving that he or she had nothing to do with the crime. It is an even more unfortunate circumstance that this is not a rare occurrence in our modern society.

Because our criminal justice system can often be flawed by attorneys' and investigators' mistakes on either side, special care must be given to records related to criminal defense investigation–particularly those records relating to serious charges in which the client was convicted. Even though a client may ultimately be convicted and sentenced to a lengthy prison term, you never know whether or not new evidence will emerge, another person will confess to the crime or (more commonly) an appeal will be granted that will send the case back to the courts trial. It is impossible to predict in advance which cases might be reopened and when; it could takes years for a court to agree to rehear a case. And in those decades, memories fade, witnesses disappear or pass away, locations change and evidence disintegrates.

For the investigators and attorneys who receive these cases years (if not decades) later, having the investigation files made by the original investigators at the time of the first trial is invaluable to their efforts to free a potentially innocent client. Interview reports with witnesses, crime scene analysis, photographs and even leads that appeared not to pan out can all play major roles in the future. For these reasons, it should be imperative upon all investigators working in criminal defense investigation to develop a separate policy for long-term retention of all records involving serious criminal cases in which a conviction was attained. We suggest employing a policy that exempts from destruction all records relating to a criminal defense investigation in which the client was convicted and was sentenced to more than 15 years. You can do this by marking closed files with a brightly-colored sticker, or simply by keeping these files separate from other retained records.

Criminal defense investigators are the only ones tasked with gathering information favorable to a client's case in the run-up to his or her original trial. The circumstances under which we conduct that investigation can never be recreated, making the documentation that we produce the best record available of the evidence as it stood during the original trial. For these reasons, we have a special responsibility to retain that evidence after a conviction in the event that new questions ever arise, so that attorneys—and the defendant—can have the best information available to challenge that conviction.

CONCLUSION

My goal in writing this book has been both to set the record straight and to help investigators who may not be as familiar with how to document a private investigation learn from my mistakes, and from the mistakes of others. Documenting an investigation in the private sector without really knowing how (coming from a law enforcement background, for example, where you may have learned to avoid creating a record of virtually anything) is like trying to cross a minefield. Many of us reach the other side—perhaps minus a limb or two—but we begrudgingly come to recognize the importance of documentation, and thereafter we never stray from the safe path again. Those who do not learn, die; they cannot cut it as private investigators. This is because at the end of every case, the only thing left is our documentation: our notes, our running resume, our reports and our statements. Surely we generate other types of evidence—video surveillance, for example—and we testify too. These things are admittedly also very important, but in this book we have argued that their importance is contingent on the context that our reports provide.

There is no reason for anyone to wade into the minefield without some guidance. I would certainly never give one of my own associates a case—no matter how experienced he or she may be—without first outlining how to document it. This book has introduced the Five Principles of Investigative Documentation and has covered everything from note-taking to document retention—essentially everything that one needs to know about how to document an investigation in the private sector. We have also deconstructed some of the common myths that investigators have about what is and is not necessary to document in an investigation. Some of these misconceptions were sparked by a misunderstanding of how technology has changed the ways that we document our cases. The fact of the matter is that documentary requirements have not changed, despite literally hundreds of technological advances that have made our investigations easier than at any other time in history.

Historically, investigations have always started with note-taking, and they still do. Also, while I confess to not knowing the origins of running resumes, I strongly suspect that some version of them has existed since the time of the first private detective agency. By sharing the same file, investigators on the same team were likely able to collaborate and share leads, under the supervision of the case manager (whether that was Eugène François Vidocq or someone else). I believe this, because we have traversed the minefield, and we know what works and what does not work.

If you take only one thing away from this book, please acknowledge that reports are the primary tangible work product of every private investigation. This, too, has been true since time immemorial, or at least as long as there have been private investigators. Not every investigator can write like a Pulitzer Prize winning author, but—whether you realized it or not before reading this book—every client *expects* you to write like a Pulitzer Prize winning author. To be taken seriously in this business, your reports have to be pristine. Using templates, a style guide and an editor can take you a long way toward this goal.

I do not purport to have invented the principles contained in this book, nor do I claim to have never fallen prey to some of the misconceptions that have also occasionally unraveled some of my colleagues' otherwise sound investigations. Like many others in this business, my methods of documentation were slipshod in the beginning, which should not be surprising, considering that none of the guidelines are clearly codified anywhere else I have ever seen. I have delighted in shredding my earlier reports in the same manner that one might look back at poems written as a teenager and cringe. Did I really profess my love to Debbie Harry? Did I really send a report to a client copied into the body of an e-mail? What seems so normal when we are inexperienced has a funny way of mortifying us later.

Thankfully, we only need to keep most of our investigative records for five years.

One of my business partners wryly pointed out that in this book I have also created a blueprint for the opposing counsel in every future case to cross-examine me and all of our associates whenever we take the stand. To this I say, if we adhere to the *Principles of Investigative Doc-*

umentation, we can all testify confidently knowing that the opposing counsel has no grounds on which to challenge our investigations, because we have crossed every t and have dotted every i.

Philip A. Becnel IV

Appendix A

INVESTIGATIVE ACRONYMS/ABBREVIATIONS

The suggested abbreviations and acronyms that are *italicized* may be used in running resumes but not in reports, and the **bolded** abbreviations may be used in both running resumes and reports. The only abbreviations that should be used in statements are those that the witness used at the time that the statement was taken.

General

> Absent Without Leave = AWOL
> About (or Approximately) = @
> Answer = A:
> Alone or in Combination = AOIC
> *Also Known As = AKA*
> **Also Known As = a/k/a**
> Applicant = APLI
> Attorney = Esq.
> Bodily Injury = BI
> Calendar Year = CY
> *Boyfriend = b/f*
> *Complaining Witness = CW*
> *Confidential Informant = CI*
> Contract = K
> Country of Birth = COB
> **Date of Birth = DOB**
> Date and Place of birth = DPOB
> Dead on Arrival = DOA
> Defendant = Δ
> *Defense Witness = ΔW*

Doing Business As = DBA
Doing Business As = d/b/a
Does not know = DK
Does not remember (or Recall) = DR
Due Diligence = DD
Fiscal Year = FY
Formerly Known As = FKA
First Name Unknown = FNU
Generally Accepted Accounting Principles = GAAP
Girlfriend = g/f
Gone on Arrival = GOA
Human Resources = HR
Important = *
Incorporation = Inc.
Intellectual Property = IP
In Question = IQ
Last Name Unknown = LNU
Law Enforcement = LE
Maiden Name = Nee
Missing Person = MP
Memorandum = MEMO
Modus Operandi = MO
No = -
Non-Consensual = NC
No Middle Initial = NMI
No Middle Name = NMN
No Response (or No Answer) = NR
Not Applicable = NA
Number = #
Physical Surveillance = FISUR
Place of Birth = POB
Plaintiff = π
Plaintiff Witness= πW
Pick up = p/u
Point (or Place) of Interest = POI
Possession = POSS
Question = Q:
Quid Pro Quo = QPQ
Respondent 1 = R1 (R2, etc.)
Report of Investigation = ROI
Separate Legal Entity = SLE
Serial Number = SN

Appendix A

Social Security Number = SSN
Special Investigations Unit = SIU
Standard Operating Procedures = SOP
Subject 1 = S1 (S2, etc.)
Trading As = T/A
Turn Around Time = TAT
Unknown Subjects = UNSUBS
Vehicle Identification Number = VIN
Witness 1 = W1 (W2, etc.)
Years Old = YO
Yes = +

*Behavioral Analysis**

Crossing arms = X-arms
Crossing legs = X-legs
Erasure = ERS
Eye contact = EC
Illustrative gesture = ILL
Latent Response = …
Real Emotion = !
Repeat Question = RQ
Shift = SFT
Smile ☺
Stop and Start Response = //
Subject Broke Eye Contact (Right) = ←
Subject Broke Eye Contact (Left) = →

Crime

Act, Intent and Motive = AIM
Assault with a Deadly Weapon = ADW
Assault with Intent to Kill = AWIK
Breaking and Entering = B&E
Carrying Deadly Weapon = CDW

---

*These symbols are useful for recording behaviors that may indicate deception or truthfulness during an interview. With the exception of symbols used to record latent and stop-and-start responses, all of these symbols should only be used in the right-hand margin of the page when taking notes-and only by investigators who have been trained to conduct behavioral analysis.

Controlled Dangerous Substance = CDS
Conviction = C̲
Dismissed = D
Distribute = DIST
Domestic Violence = DV
Driving Under the Influence = DUI
Driving While Intoxicated = DWI
Driving Without License = DWL
Driving While Suspended = DWS
Gunshot Wound = GSW
Racketeer Influenced and Corrupt Organizations Act = RICO

Days of the Week

Sunday = SUN
Monday = MON
Tuesday = TUES
Wednesday = WED
Thursday = THURS
Friday = FRI
Saturday = SAT

Description

Age, Sex, Location = ASL
Asian Female = AF
Asian Male = AM
Black = BLK
Black Female = BF
Black Male = BM
Blonde = BLD
Blue = BLU
Brown = BRN
Eastbound = EB
Feet = '
Female (General) = F
Hispanic Female = HF
Hispanic Male = HM
Inches = "
Green = GRN
Male (general) = M

Appendix A 81

Northbound = NB
Purple = PUR
Red = RD
Southbound = SB
Westbound = WB
White = WHT
Yellow = YLW

Government and Organizations

Department of Agriculture = USDA
U.S. Air Force = USAF
Bureau of Alcohol, Tobacco and Firearms = ATF
American Bar Association = ABA
American Civil Liberties Union = ACLU
Assistant U.S. Attorney = AUSA
Bureau of Citizenship and Immigration Services = USCIS
Central Intelligence Agency = CIA
U.S. Coast Guard = USCG
Commodity Futures Trading Commission = CFTC
Department of Defense = DOD
Defense Intelligence Agency = DIA
Department of Corrections = DOC
Drug Enforcement Administration = DEA
Department of Education = DOED
Department of Energy = DOE
Environmental Protection Agency = EPA
Federal Aviation Administration = FAA
Federal Bureau of Investigation = FBI
Federal Communications Commission = FCC
Federal Deposit Insurance Corporation = FDIC
General Accounting Office = GAO
General Services Administration = GSA
Government (General) = GOVT
Department of Health and Human Services = HHS
Department of Housing and Urban Development = HUD
Internal Revenue Service = IRS
Agency for International Development = USAID
Department of Justice = DOJ
Department of Labor = DOL
U.S. Marshal Service = USMS

U.S. Marine Corps = USMC
Military (General) = MIL
Department of Motor Vehicles = DMV
National Aeronautics and Space Administration = NASA
National Crime Information Center = NCIC
National Labor Relations Board = NLRB
National Science Foundation = NSI
National Security Agency = NSA
Non-Governmental Organization = NGO
Nuclear Regulatory Commission = NRC
Office of Personnel Management = OPM
Police Department (General) = PD
U.S. Postal Service = USPS
U.S. Secret Service = USSS
Social Security Administration = SSA
Special Police Officer = SPO
Special Agent = SA
Special Agent in Charge = SAC
State Police (General) = SPOL
Department of Transportation = DOT
Department of Veterans Affairs = VA
White House = WH
World Health Organization = WHO

Laws and Legal Terminology

Administrative Law Judge = ALJ
Americans with Disabilities Act = ADA
Age Discrimination in Employment Act = ADEA
Bankruptcy = BKTCY
Collective Bargaining Agreement = CBA
Charging Party = CP
Copyright Matter = ©
Civil Rights Act = CRA
Civil Protective Order = CPO
Defendant = Δ
Defense Counsel = ΔC
U.S. District Court = USDC
Emergency Protective Order = EPO
Equal Employment Opportunity Commission = EEOC
Employee Retirement Income Security Act = ERISA
Employee Polygraph Protection Act = EPPA

Equal Credit Opportunity Act = ECOA
Electronic Communications Privacy Act = ECPA
Foreign Corrupt Practices Act = FCPA
Fair Debt Collections Practices Act = FDCP
Fair Labor Standards Act = FLSA
False Claims Act = FCA
Family Medical Leave Act = FMLA
Freedom of Information Act = FOIA
Judgment = J
Motion for Summary Judgment = MSJ
Nolo Contendere = NC
Nolle Prosequi = NP
Opposing Counsel = OC
Plaintiff = π
Plaintiff's Counsel = πC
Power of Attorney = POA
Probation Before Judgment = PBJ
Occupational Safety and Health Act = OSHA
Sarbanes-Oxley Act = SOX

States and Territories

Alabama = AL
Alaska = AK
American Samoa = AS
Arizona = AZ
Arkansas = AR
California = CA
Colorado = CO
Connecticut = CT
Delaware = DE
District of Columbia = Washington, DC
Federated States of Micronesia = FM
Florida = FL
Georgia = GA
Guam = GU
Hawaii = HI
Idaho = ID
Illinois = IL
Indiana = IN
Iowa = IA
Kansas = KS

Kentucky = KY
Louisiana = LA
Maine = ME
Marshal Islands = MH
Maryland = MD
Massachusetts = MA
Michigan = MI
Minnesota = MN
Mississippi = MS
Missouri = MO
Montana = MT
Nebraska = NE
Nevada = NV
New Hampshire = NH
New Jersey = NJ
New Mexico = NM
New York = NY
North Carolina = NC
North Dakota = ND
Northern Mariana Islands = MP
Ohio = OH
Oklahoma = OK
Oregon = OR
Palau = PW
Pennsylvania = PA
Puerto Rico = PR
Rhode Island = RI
South Carolina = SC
South Dakota = SD
Tennessee = TN
Texas = TX
Utah = UT
Vermont = VT
Virgin Islands = VI
Virginia = VA
Washington = WA
West Virginia = WV
Wisconsin = WI
Wyoming = WY

Appendix B

SAMPLE REPORTS

In-Person Interview Status Report

ATTORNEY WORK PRODUCT

INVESTIGATIVE REPORT

DATE: DECEMBER 23, 2010

FROM: THOMAS MAGNUM (TSM)

TO: MARY MORSTAN

CC: JOE BRODY

CASE NAME: ABC PROPERTY MANAGEMENT (10-0001)

With reference to the above case, we interviewed Hal Kines, SSN unknown, DOB unknown, on December 12, 2009, by meeting with him at the ABC Property Management office located at 1814 Massachusetts Ave., NW, Washington, DC 20036. Kines is a residential maintenance supervisor for Acme Services, which performs maintenance at this and other ABC Property Management properties, which include several commercial and residential buildings in and around Washington, DC. Kines is described as a white male, approximately 5 feet, 11 inches tall, with a medium build and thinning, brown hair. He has a tattoo of an eagle on his outer, left forearm.

After being advised of the identity of the interviewer and the nature of the investigation, Kines agreed to be interviewed regarding the matter of thefts and controls at ABC Property Management and told us the following:

Kines stated that he had no prior knowledge of the theft or what John Dalmas stole. He said that the maintenance unit at ABC Property Management functioned on "99.9 percent trust." He said that, after Dalmas's theft, ABC Property Management suspended service on its residential properties when an ABC Property Management supervisor was not present, and this effectively took him "out of the equation," since there is no system in place for ABC Property Management supervisors to visit these locations.

Asked how long he has worked for Acme Services, Kines said that it was his fourth year on October 11, 2008. Asked if he has always had the same job there, he said that he has, and that he is a maintenance supervisor. Asked about his coworkers when he started, he said that Dalmas worked there and had been there for approximately one year. Asked if Dalmas did the same job as he, Kines said that Dalmas was also a maintenance supervisor. Asked if Dalmas was his supervisor, Kines said that Dalmas was his supervisor, but this was only because Acme Services wanted to "label" everything, and because Dalmas had been there one year longer. Kines said that Dalmas had the electrical experience, where he (Kines) had the locksmith experience, so the two men complemented one another in terms of their expertise.

Asked if he and Dalmas generally worked together on work orders, Kines said that they did not work together and would routinely go off on their own to complete their work orders. He said, however, that he and Dalmas worked together for the spring and fall inspections on the Connecticut Avenue property and made sure everything worked properly. He said that they checked the bathrooms, drains, and anything that might be wrong in the units. He explained that they divided up the orders and took care of them separately-typically five to 10 work orders a day, but sometimes as many as 20. Kines said that the inspections were the only instances where they worked together. He added, however, that he sometimes assisted Dalmas if he had an electrical question or needed help removing a toilet. He said that they both know electrical work, and Dalmas has a few certificates in electrical work.

Asked who worked with him when he started, Kines said that it was the same people who still work at ABC Property Management. Asked if he liked working there when he started, Kines said that he loved the job and still loves it. He explained that the work is not redundant; there is always something different. He said that he likes the people and the environment. He added that he and Dalmas hit it off, too.

Kines said that he used to work for another management company that contracted to ABC Property Management for a year before they lost their contract, at which point Acme Services won the contract and they hired him. He said that the name of the company was FGT (phonetic) and that it was an outsourced maintenance company.

Asked what he did on November 1, 2009, Kines said that it was a routine day, and he took care of maintenance orders at the Connecticut Ave. property. He said that he could not remember anything that day and that it was "kind of gray." Asked what he did on November 9, he said that he came in to the same location and there was a "commotion," which he described as whispering and people talking about the night before. He estimated that he came in between 7:30 and 7:50 a.m. and said that he first spoke to Mary Bellamy, who was going about her usual activities at the front desk. He said that she was discussing why the police officers' arrival was not written in the log.

Kines explained, until Bellamy told him, he was unaware that the police had come to the ABC Property Management office the night before. He added that any emergency is required to be logged into an orange book at the front and that Bellamy and Owen Taylor were discussing why the arrival was not in the book. He said that no one else was present at that time. He said that Bellamy and Taylor told him about the incident and that Mr. (Jack) Williams told them to leave it out of the red book. He said that other incidents requiring the police occasionally occur on the premises, such as boyfriend/girlfriend conflicts, drunkenness or renovations occurring through improper channels and that this happens once or twice per month.

Kines said that, at this point, no one knew why the police had been called, and they were all trying to guess what had happened. He said that they talked about people being drunk or having sex on the roof deck. He said that he was up at the front desk when two uniformed police officers came back, and this was after approximately 15 to 30 minutes of discussing the incident with the other employees. Asked if he had considered theft as a possible reason for the police to be called, he said that he had not. He said that the two uniformed officers asked if Chester Wheeler was downstairs.

Asked if he had left the front desk area between the time he arrived at work and the time the officers arrived, Kines said that he did not leave until later, when he went to have breakfast. He said that he clocks in at the front desk. He said that the two officers went upstairs, and then Wheeler came downstairs. Kines said that they told Wheeler that police officers went upstairs to look for him. Kines said Wheeler then went outside to the police cars to wait for them. The officers came back down, he said, and talked to Wheeler for approximately 10 minutes. Kines said that they pulled out a DVD and played it on a laptop, then came inside to look at the laptop in the lobby. He said that he stayed at the front desk while all of this happened.

Kines added that the tenant and the officers used Charlotte Manning's laptop to view the DVD, which Manning pulled out of her backpack. Kines explained that Manning is one of ABC Bank's branch managers and happens to also reside in the building. He said that Manning came out and waited by the door for Wheeler and the officers, and then Wheeler, Manning and the officers went into William's office.

Asked when he had breakfast, Kines said that he had breakfast after Manning, Wheeler and the officers went downstairs. Kines estimated that, at this point, he had spent 45 to 60 minutes at the front desk.

Asked about Dalmas, Kines said that the building had problems with the heat, so Dalmas went to the eighth floor to check the hot water. He said that Dalmas did not arrive through the front door; otherwise, Kines thought, Wheeler would have seen Dalmas and called the police. Kines said that he did not see Dalmas arrive that day. He explained that when Dalmas was late, Dalmas would arrive through the back entrance, as that was the most direct route from the Metro. Kines said that Dalmas normally came in later than him and stayed later.

Asked when he saw Dalmas that day, Kines said that, when he came out of the shop, Dalmas called him, and he told Dalmas that the police were here out front of the building. At this point, Kines said, Dalmas told him that he was going upstairs to check the water temperature and told Kines that he was in the garage. Kines said that he then went to meet Dalmas in the garage and that this occurred around the same time that he had breakfast. Kines said that Dalmas told him some of the tenants were complaining that they did not have sufficient hot water.

Asked if he told Dalmas that Wheeler had been speaking to the police, Kines said that he did not remember mentioning Wheeler and just told Dalmas that the police were there. Kines said that Dalmas replied that he was going upstairs to check on the hot water issue. Kines estimated that Dalmas's first phone call to him took place around 10 a.m. and said that he went down to meet Dalmas right after the call. Asked if call records would demonstrate this, Kines said that he could not remember if Dalmas called or "chirped" him. Kines said that he thought Dalmas called him, because he believes he tried to chirp Dalmas and that Dalmas then called him back.

Kines said that the ABC Property Management supervisors, including Manning, plus Williams, Pat Chambers (female) and the police officers were in the management office, and he (Kines) tried to listen to what they were saying by hanging around by the stairs near Chambers' office. He said that Chambers was in her office, and finally the group that was talking came out and asked him where Dalmas was.

Kines said that he was in the shop when Dalmas called.

Kines added that, when Dalmas is late, Dalmas does not punch in but instead writes his time in on the time card.

Asked what happened next, Kines said that the female officer asked where Dalmas was and that he told her that Dalmas was on the eighth floor. He said that she asked him to call Dalmas, so he chirped Dalmas, and Dalmas called him back. He said that he asked Dalmas where he was, and Dalmas told him that he was on the rooftop. He continued by saying that, when they went up to the roof to look for Dalmas, Dalmas was not there. Kines said that they looked for him and then came back downstairs.

Kines said that he asked the police if they thought it was Dalmas. Asked what the statement, "it was [Dalmas]," meant, Kines said that when he was asked where Dalmas was, he asked them, "Did they think it was him?" He said that he inferred Dalmas's involvement in something, but he did not know at that time what Dalmas had actually done. Kines said he was then told by one of the police officers that they had a video of Dalmas "putting stuff up his shirt."

Asked what happened next, Kines said that he went back to the shop and that his "mind was going everywhere." He said that he came back to talk to Chambers and that he told her that they were looking for Dalmas. He said that Chambers got teary-eyed and looked surprised. He said that she told him she never thought the police were there for Dalmas. Asked when this conversation occurred, Kines said it was before lunch.

Asked if he talked to Dalmas again that day, Kines said that Dalmas called him approximately 20 to 30 minutes later and that Dalmas sounded out of breath. He said that he and Dalmas spoke after he (Kines) left Chambers' office. Kines said that he had been talking to Chambers for about 15 to 20 minutes. Asked how long the officers had been in the lobby, Kines said that he did not know. He said that Dalmas told him that he ran because he has two DUI charges in Virginia and did not want his name to be run in the criminal database.

Asked if he told Dalmas what the police had said, Kines said that he told Dalmas that the police had a video of him. He said that this conversation lasted five to seven minutes, mostly because there were long pauses in the conversation. He said that he told Dalmas that he had "screwed himself." He explained that Dalmas had been going to school for a Class 3 engineer's license and will no longer be able to do that type of work.

Asked if anyone was present when Dalmas called the second time, Kines said no one was present. Asked where he was when he received the call, Kines said that he was in the shop but walked to the garage in order to get service. He said that no one else was in the shop or the garage. Dalmas called him again, he added, when Dalmas got home. Kines said that Dalmas told him that he was at home and that his wife "will be pissed." He said that he told Dalmas that Chambers left because she was crying. He said that he asked Dalmas why he stole the money and DVDs, as he makes a fairly good salary at Acme Services.

Asked if Dalmas admitted to taking the money and DVDs, Kines said that after he told Dalmas that the officers have a video of him, Dalmas said, "Dude, I don't know why I did that," and also said that he had not been himself. Kines explained that Dalmas quit smoking and had been taking a medication called Chantix. Kines said that he observed Dalmas's mood change; in particular, Dalmas became more aggressive. Kines said that Dalmas told him that he took the money and put the DVDs in a black trash bag in the trash room. Kines told us that the trash room is located in the large garage, which is the same garage where he and Dalmas met that morning. He said that Dalmas told him the bag was by the side of the trash can.

Kines said that he talked to Williams, who asked him if he would be able to get the money and DVDs back. Kines said that it was at this point that he asked Dalmas where the money and DVDs were located, at which point he walked away from Williams and was once again alone while on the phone with Dalmas. Asked why he thought Dalmas called him, Kines said that he thought Dalmas might have felt stupid about what happened. He said that Dalmas asked him if the police were still there, to which Kines replied that he did not know, as he was then downstairs. Kines said that he and Dalmas did not discuss anything else. Asked about the length of this conversation, he said that he does not know, but Dalmas called him again several times that day, approximately six to seven more times. Kines explained that the high number of calls was because some of the phone calls dropped.

Asked how long these other conversations were (the ones that were not dropped), Kines said that some were rather long, as he and Dalmas discussed work-related matters, such as the shop codes for the generator on Connecticut Ave. and the desk phone, in order for Kines to be able to retrieve messages for maintenance orders. He said that they also discussed account numbers for Home Depot.

Asked if he saw Dalmas with a bag on November 10, 2009, Kines said that Dalmas was carrying an army bag, which he carried every day. Asked if he saw Dalmas carrying a black trash bag, Kines said that he did not. Asked why Dalmas was carrying his army bag in the garage after he had already arrived to work, Kines said that he does not know, but perhaps Dalmas was planning on leaving. Kines said that he did not consider it unusual at the time, but in retrospect it seems unusual.

Asked if he has seen Dalmas since November 10, 2009, Kines said that he has not. Asked if he has spoken to Dalmas since then, he said that he has and that they have talked about whether the police were trying to get anyone else and generally what has been happening. He said that the last time he spoke to Dalmas was approximately seven to nine days ago and that neither man has discussed the November 10 incident since the day it happened. He also said that he has since been advised by Acme Services and ABC Property Management not to talk to Dalmas anymore.

Asked if he noticed anything else suspicious, Kines said that nothing else stood out. Asked if he was surprised when he found out Dalmas took the money and DVDs from Wheeler's condo, he said that he was shocked and cried about it, because he was upset that Dalmas had "screwed his life" over stealing "porn DVDs." He said that he knows that Dalmas now cannot get hired anywhere.

Asked why Dalmas did not take the DVDs with him on the night of November 9, 2010, Kines said that he does not know. Asked if Dalmas showed him the pornographic DVDs, Kines said Dalmas did not. Asked if he ever watched pornography on the computer, Kines first denied but then admitted to watching pornography on the computer under his login.

Asked how he knows that the DVDs Dalmas stole from Wheeler were pornographic, Kines said that Dalmas told him during one of their phone conversations. He said that a male police officer also told him in the elevator downstairs, after they had looked for Dalmas on the roof deck, that Dalmas stole pornographic DVDs. Kines said that Dalmas later confirmed on the phone that he stole approximately 10 pornographic DVDs and that they were in the trash room.

Note: This completes this investigative report, prepared by TSM and reviewed by Philip Marlowe, both investigators for Dinolt Becnel & Wells Investigative Group LLC, online at www.dinolt.com.

Telephone Interview Status Report

ATTORNEY WORK PRODUCT

INVESTIGATIVE REPORT

DATE: JULY 12, 2008

FROM: ARTHUR CONAN DOYLE (ACD)

TO: GEORGE KALECKI

CC: JAMES DODD

CASE NAME: ARTHUR RICKERBY (08-0001)

With reference to the above, I interviewed Ian Murdoch, SSN unknown, DOB unknown, on July 9, 2008, by calling phone number 805-555-7419.

After being advised of the identity of the interviewer and the nature of the investigation, Murdoch agreed to be interviewed regarding the matter of Arthur Rickerby and told me the following:

Murdoch is currently the law enforcement sales representative for the Commonwealth of Virginia for Acme Firearms. Asked if he is the only sales representative for law enforcement in Virginia, Murdoch said that he is.

Murdoch "officially" began working as an Acme Firearms employee on October 1, 2007, after being a paid consultant for Acme Firearms since July 2007. It was Rickerby who interviewed and ultimately assisted in hiring Murdoch to that position, according to Murdoch.

Prior to working with Acme Firearms, Murdoch was a sergeant with the Roanoke City Police Department for nearly 16 years and a deputy with the Fairfax County Sheriff's Department for five years. He first met Rickerby in the early 1990s when the two were working together with the Roanoke City Police Department.

Asked if he retained the e-mail that was sent to Acme Firearms employees from Laura Knapp announcing that Rickerby was on administrative leave, Murdoch said that he did. Asked if he would send a copy of that e-mail to us, Murdoch said that he would.

Asked if he had any opinion or emotion about Rickerby after reading that e-mail, Murdoch said that it elicited a strong reaction from him.

"Hell yeah I had an opinion about it, it pissed me off," Murdoch said. "When I saw that e-mail the first thing that came to my mind was that maybe there was a family emergency or someone got sick, I could never think right off the bat that this would be something negative against him [Rickerby]."

Shortly after receiving the e-mail, Murdoch called Rickerby to find out if everything was all right. Rickerby responded by informing Murdoch of the incident involving the U.S. Secret Service and the firearm accessories.

Asked how this made him feel when he learned about the incident, Murdoch said that it really bothered him.

"I was furious, that's bullshit," Murdoch said. "As a law enforcement officer, you're taught and trained to do something when people break the law, and when you report something like this to your boss, they shouldn't retaliate against you. They can't retaliate against you. That is against the law."

"Ever since then, things haven't been the same for him, and I'm just really pissed off about it," Murdoch said.

Asked how things are not the same for Rickerby since he was placed on administrative leave, Murdoch said that he had felt that Rickerby had been mistreated by Acme Firearms.

Asked for an example of this, Murdoch said that since Rickerby was placed on administrative leave, he very rarely sees Rickerby's e-mail address copied on company e-mails that would normally pertain to him. Asked for more examples, Murdoch said that he remembers just hearing from people like John Watson that Rickerby was being mistreated around the office. Murdoch said that since he is in the Virginia area and not Chicago, his first-hand knowledge of these incidents is limited.

Murdoch added that it was now considered a growing concern among some of the employees at Acme Firearms that the Acme Firearms executives were "ganging up" on the employees with law enforcement backgrounds, partially as a result of this situation.

"I'm concerned about my position with the company as well now," Murdoch said. "No one's said anything like, 'After Arthur [Rickerby] leaves, you're gone too,' but me and the rest of the law enforcement guys, we're worried about our jobs."

Asked if he has any specific examples or evidence of this, Murdoch said that it was just "a feeling that we have."

Murdoch checked with Sam Merton at the Fairfax County Sheriff's Department firing range and determined that it was not him who had mentioned Rickerby to Murdoch. While he had not been able to reach Victor Trevor, Murdoch said that he was now "pretty sure" that it was Trevor who mentioned Rickerby's situation to him on the phone.

Asked if he could remember exactly what Trevor said, Murdoch said, "just, 'Hey, I heard that Arthur [Rickerby] is not at Acme Firearms, that he was put on administrative leave, what did he do?'"

The fact that one person is stating that another person is on administrative leave always holds a negative connotation in the world of law enforcement, Murdoch said.

"When you hear that someone's on administrative leave, you know something is wrong," Murdoch said. "In law enforcement, it's always something negative, or criminal–that you're the subject of an ongoing internal investigation. It's never anything good."

Asked if he can remember the exact date that the police asked about Rickerby's administrative leave, Murdoch said that he could not remember the exact date, but that it happened within one or two days after Knapp's announcement of Rickerby's status.

Murdoch said that we should be able to determine a more specific time period after we look at when the e-mail was sent out.

Interview Refusal Report

ATTORNEY WORK PRODUCT

INVESTIGATIVE REPORT

DATE: MARCH 18, 2011

FROM: VINCENT HANNA (VH)

TO: MONTGOMERY BROGAN

CC:

CASE NAME: JIM JOHNSON

With reference to the above case, I attempted to interview Neil McCauley, SSN unknown, DOB unknown, at approximately 6:30 p.m. on March 17, 2011 at his home, located at 2181 Applegate Lane, Silver Spring, Maryland 20741. McCauley is described as a white male, approximately 50-years-old, about 5 feet 10 inches tall, with silver hair and a goatee.

After being advised of the identity of the interviewer and the nature of the investigation, McCauley declined to be interviewed regarding the matter of Jim Johnson and Bridgeway Computers and told me the following:

McCauley told me that he worked with Johnson when Johnson arrived at Bridgeway in March 2007, but the two never had much contact.

McCauley then said, "That is all I have to tell you, now please get off my property." He then abruptly walked through his garage and entered his home.

This completes this investigative report, prepared by VH and reviewed by Osborne Cox, both investigators for Dinolt Becnel & Wells Investigative Group LLC, online at www.dinolt.com.

Appendix B

Due Diligence Concluding Report

ATTORNEY WORK PRODUCT

INVESTIGATIVE REPORT

DATE: JANUARY 30, 2009

FROM: SIMON TEMPLER (SUT)

TO: JOE CAIRO

CC:

CASE NAME: ABC BANK (09-0001)

We were asked to find out if the owners of Acme Travels, LLP can pay a $1 million judgment and to confirm that Myrna Devlin and James Moriarty live at 701 Berrywood Lane, Great Falls, Virginia 22066.

The officers and potential owners of Acme Travels are:

- Myrna Devlin
  DOB April 17, 1902
  SSN 123-45-6789

- James Moriarty
  DOB February 1, 1897
  SSN unknown

- William Legrand
  DOB September 16, 1911
  SSN 987-65-4321

Summary:

Devlin, Moriarty and Legrand probably cannot collectively pay a $1 million judgment. According to property records, Devlin and Moriarty appear to currently live at 701 Berrywood Lane, Great Falls, Virginia 22066.

Legrand has little to no equity in his property. Devlin still has outstanding judgments against her and does not appear to own any property. Moriarty may have several hundred thousand dollars in equity as a result of her recent marriage to Miles Archer. That said, since marrying Moriarty, a guardianship case has been brought on behalf of Miles Archer in Prince George's County Circuit Court.

It appears as though several of Archer's recent business transactions were designed to benefit Devlin and Moriarty.

Myrna Devlin:

According to credit header information, Virginia driver license information and an August 2008 lease (discussed below), Devlin lives at 701 Berrywood Lane, Great Falls, Virginia 22066. If she has left this address, she may live with Sam Merton, DOB July 29, 1922, at 2523 Dulles Station Boulevard, Apartment 101, Herndon, Virginia 20171.

Devlin had an Individual Real Estate License in Virginia, but it expired on October 31, 2008.

She does not appear to own any property, and there is an outstanding judgment against her in Fairfax County Circuit Court for $21,000. Devlin was delinquent in her personal rent when she lived at 7864 Tennyson Drive, McLean, Virginia 22101.

She owned a 2000 Buick LeSabre, but it was demolished in 2009.

James Moriarty:

According to a marriage certificate and court filings in the guardianship case for Miles Archer, Moriarty lives at 701 Berrywood Lane, Great Falls, Virginia 22066. As discussed below, she married Archer in November 2008. Prior to the marriage, Archer bought 701 Berrywood Lane, Great Falls, Virginia 22066 for $1.45 million with a mortgage for $660,000. The property currently assesses for $1.395 million. Rich also owns a property in Prince George's County that assesses for $248,100.

Shortly after Moriarty and Archer married, a guardianship case was brought on behalf of Archer. In February 2009, the judge in the case signed an order giving guardianship to Mary Morstan and attorney Laura Knapp. Moriarty has contested the guardianship, and the case is still ongoing.

On November 30, 2010, Investigator Amy Midkiff attempted to retrieve Archer's guardianship case from Prince George's County Family Court and was told the case is under seal. It may be worth attempting to interview Archer's personal and financial guardians. Please let us know if you would like us to contact them.

According to archives of *The Washington Examiner*, on September 19, 2009, a trust sale for 701 Berrywood Lane was posted in the newspaper. It does not appear as though any foreclosure proceedings have been brought against the property. Archer is still listed as the owner.

William Legrand:

According to his Facebook page, Legrand, retired as a federal attorney in 2005 and recently launched several unnamed business ventures. According to online public records, he was an Attorney Examiner for the U.S. Department of Labor, Office of the Judicial Officer. A person named William Legrand is registered with the DC Bar. No contact information is given for this individual, but he is listed as a "Judicial" member.

Legrand owns 6001 Lupine Lane, McLean, Virginia 22101. In 2006, he refinanced his mortgage for $1,004,500. Also in 2006, he was given a $200,000 credit line. The property currently assesses for $1,093,760.

According to Virginia Department of Motor Vehicle records, Legrand owns a 1995 Nissan Altima, License Plate Number 945-DER, and a 2006 Ford Escort, License Plate Number GAD-2227.

On February 4, 2009, Acme Farms Build LLC was registered in Virginia with its principal and registered agent address listed as Legrand's house. A person named Richie Cole is listed as the company's registered agent.

Acme Travels:

There is presently no Virginia-registered company with the name Acme Travels, LLP. Acme Travels *LLC* was registered in Virginia on August 12, 2008 and lists Myrna Devlin as its registered agent. Her address is listed as 571 Maple Avenue West, Suite 209, Vienna, Virginia 22180. Acme Travels' principal address is listed as 701 Berrywood Lane, Great Falls, Virginia 22066. The company is delinquent in paying its filing fees to the Secretary of State.

The company was registered several months after the lease was signed with ABC Bank.

Potential Fraud Timeline:

August 14, 2008 Devlin and Miles Archer signed a lease and option to purchase agreement on behalf of Berrywood Manor LLC. Devlin and Archer are listed as managers of Berrywood Manor in the contract. Devlin and Archer formed Berrywood Manors to acquire 701 Berrywood Lane and to operate an assisted living facility on the property with Devlin as the manager. Archer, Berrywood Manor and Devlin are all listed as co-occupants under this lease. Berrywood and Devlin are jointly and severally liable for the rent that covers both the mortgage and real estate taxes. The contract also gives Devlin and Berrywood Manor a right to purchase the property for the price paid by Archer plus the closing costs.

Additionally the contract states that:

> Whereas, Archer may have to purchase the property individually at the end of the month as Berrywood Manor is not yet in a financial position to take title, and the parties wish to insure that their general understanding of what is to happen is reflected in this agreement in the event of the death of Archer before that transfer of the property to Berrywood Manor is complete.

Pat Chambers, who is a real estate agent in the same office as Devlin, notarized this contract.

August 29, 2009 Berrywood Manor LLC was registered in Virginia. This is the same day Acme Travels LLC was registered. Archer is listed as the registered agent at 701 Berrywood Lane, Great Falls, Virginia 22066. This address is also listed as the principal address for the company.

September 1, 2009 Archer purchased 701 Berrywood Lane, Great Falls, Virginia 22066 for $1,450,000.[*] Rich signed the deed on August 28, 2008. The notary on the deed is listed as James Dodd. According to the Virginia State Bar, Dodd is a member of the Virginia State Bar with 571 Maple Avenue West, Suite 209, Vienna, Virginia 22180 listed as his address. This is the same address that is listed for Devlin in the Acme Travels registration. According to Re/Max's web site and the Acme Travles lease, Devlin works as a real estate agent in Suite 306 of the same building.[†]

---

[*] He was given a 40-year mortgage for $660,000 with a 5.625 percent interest rate, which makes the monthly payment $3,460.
[†] I found an advertisement for an open house for the property in January 2009. Richie Cole of Weichert Realtors, telephone 703-555-2219, was showing it. The asking price at the time was $1,699,000.

Berrywood Manor is not listed as an assisted-living facility in the Virginia Department of Social Services database.

The deed for the property contains a home occupancy-rider, which requires Archer to make the property his primary residency. The property appears to be a single-family home. We have not researched the zoning restrictions for the property.

November 4, 2009 Archer married Moriarty in Fairfax County. It was a civil ceremony performed by Chester Wheeler of 9115 Union Mill Road, Clifton, Virginia 20124. Archer and Moriarty's address on the marriage certificate is listed as 701 Berrywood Lane, Great Falls, Virginia 22066. Also, according to the marriage certificate, this was Moriarty's third marriage.

November 25, 2009 Owen Taylor filed a petition in Prince George's County Family Court for appointment of guardianship over Archer's and his property.

February 19, 2010 Morstan was appointed guardian of Archer, and Knapp was appointed guardian of Archer's property.

March 5, 2010 Devlin filed a motion to alter, amend and vacate the February 19, 2009 order for the removal of Morstan as the guardian of Archer. The case is still open.

Other additional info:

According to a public records database, the mobile phone number listed for Devlin in the Acme Travels lease, 703-555-1937, is registered to Archer.

Note: This completes this investigative report, prepared SUT, an investigator with Dinolt Becnel & Wells Investigative Group LLC, and it was reviewed by James Bond of Dinolt (UK) Ltd.

Background Check Report

ATTORNEY WORK PRODUCT

INVESTIGATIVE REPORT

DATE: AUGUST 28, 2011

FROM: DALE DENTON (DD)

TO: MICHAEL CLAYTON

CC:

CASE NAME: CIRCUIT WORLD APPLIANCES

With reference to the above, I was tasked with conducting a background investigation regarding Robert Doback, SSN 999-99-9999, DOB 02/28/1971. The following details the results of my investigation:

According to credit header information, since 1997, Doback has lived in Washtenaw, Saginaw, Wayne and Genesee counties, Michigan; Merrimack County, New Hampshire; Windham County, Vermont; Middlesex County, Massachusetts; and Kings County, New York.

No federal cases were found pertaining to Doback.

No criminal cases were found in Michigan pertaining to Doback.

In 2001, in the District Court for Merrimack County, New Hampshire, in civil contract Case Number 41-Cv01-2248, Ridgeway Golf, Inc. v. Doback, a consent judgment of $2,571 was entered in favor of Ridgeway Golf, Inc., along with almost $3,100 in attorney fees.

In 2004, 2005 and 2007, Allison Huff filed domestic violence charges against Doback in Kings County, New York.

On July 17, 2008, in the Supreme Court for Kings County, New York, in criminal Case Number 2008KN06891, Doback pleaded guilty to second degree menacing, a Class A misdemeanor, and was sentenced to one year of probation, a suspended sentence of six months and seven days of community service. The complaining witness in the case was Allison Huff. Doback was originally charged with felony second degree assault. The case was satisfied on July 18, 2009.

No civil or criminal cases were found in Windham County, Vermont pertaining to Doback since 1997.

No civil or criminal cases were found in Middlesex County, Massachusetts pertaining to Doback since 1997.

Surveillance Status Report

ATTORNEY WORK PRODUCT

INVESTIGATIVE REPORT

DATE: JUNE 19, 2006

FROM: THOMAS MAGNUM (TSM)

TO: JOHN WATSON

CC: EFFIE PERNIE

CASE NAME: ABC BANK (06-0003)

With reference to the above, we were tasked with conducting surveillance as to the whereabouts of Casper Gutman, SSN unknown, DOB December 25, 1937. A description and residential address of the subject were provided to assist in our investigation. Gutman is a white male, approximately 6 feet 2 inches tall, weighing approximately 250 pounds.

Additionally, prior to initiating the surveillance, we conducted an independent investigation regarding Gutman. As part of this investigation, we determined that Gutman: owns a 2000 Ford Explorer bearing Maryland Tag Number M945571; resides at 3500 Mapleview Court, Odenton, Maryland 21113; and uses telephone number (410) 555-1912, which is registered to a separate address, 1010 Eastham Court, Crofton, Maryland 21114.

We also determined that Gutman's wife is Brigid O'Shaughnessy, SSN unknown, DOB January 15, 1921. Our investigation determined that O'Shaughnessy is approximately 5 feet 5 inches in height and weighs 170 pounds, and she drives a 2001 four-door Chevy sedan bearing Maryland Tag Number 3ABG98.

On June 12, 2006, at approximately 3:15 p.m., I arrived at the Eastham Court address, where I did not see Gutman's vehicle or any other sign of the subject. The front door of the apartment and the mail boxes were unremarkable. In an effort to determine if Gutman's phone rang to this location, I dialed the aforementioned telephone number from a blocked number while standing in the hallway of the building, and I could not hear the phone ringing inside of the apartment. Through the phone, I heard a man's voice on the voice mail message.

On the same date, at approximately 4:10 p.m., I arrived at the Mapleview address, where I witnessed Gutman's vehicle parked in front of his townhouse. I observed the townhouse while seated in my vehicle from a distance of approximately 100 feet. The shades of the home were drawn shut, and I noted no movement inside the home. After surreptitiously placing a penny on the passenger-side rear tire of the Ford Exploer, I then left the area at approximately 4:30 p.m. and returned again at about 4:50 p.m.

On the same date, at approximately 5:30 p.m., I witnessed an individual matching Gutman's description, wearing a hat and sunglasses exit the townhouse and get into his vehicle. I proceeded to follow the subject at a distance of approximately 1,500 feet. After traveling less than a mile, I witnessed the subject make a sharp left from Strawberry Lake Way onto Apple Blossom Court, and I proceeded southbound on Strawberry Lake Way, passing Apple Blossom Court. Within less than a minute, Gutman—while traveling at a high rate of speed—then turned back onto Strawberry Lake Way and pulled up behind my vehicle. I made a right onto Streamview Drive and parked in a residential area. As I exited my vehicle, the subject pulled up to where I was standing and rolled down his window. Feigning like I assumed he was going to ask me for directions, I greeted him in a friendly manner. After returning my greeting, the subject rolled up his window but remained seated in his car approximately 15 feet from my location, while I spoke to an unknown woman in the doorway of a nearby townhouse (telling her that I was looking for my lost dog), at which point Gutman drove away.

I then returned to an area where I could observe a traffic circle on Strawberry Lake Way, near Gutman's home, where I waited until the arrival of a second investigator on the scene. I noted no significant activity during this timeframe, although I could not observe the subject's home from my location.

Investigator Jane Moneypenny arrived on the same date at approximately 6:50 p.m., and together, in Moneypenny's vehicle, we returned to an area approximately 1,200 feet and within eyesight of Gutman's home. At this time, we witnessed both the subject's and O'Shaughnessy's vehicles parked near the townhouse. The door to the townhouse was open, and we observed a white and brown, medium-sized dog through the glass of the outer door.

On the same date at about 7 p.m., we observed a woman matching O'Shaughnessy's description exit the townhouse, enter her vehicle and leave the area. At approximately 7:35 p.m., O'Shaughnessy returned to the home, and she then left again at 7:45 p.m., before returning again at 8:25 p.m.

On the same date, at approximately 10:40 p.m., Moneypenny placed a penny on the rear passenger-side tire of the Ford Explorer, and we ceased the surveillance for the evening.

On June 14 2006, Moneypenny returned to the Mapleview Court address at approximately 6:55 a.m., when she observed that the subject's vehicle was no longer parked in front of the house. She noted that there were two pennies located in the parking spot where the subject's vehicle had previously been parked. The Chevy, however, was still there. Moneypenny took up a position approximately 1,200 feet from the subject's home.

On the same date, at approximately 8:20 a.m., Moneypenny observed O'Shaughnessy walking the same dog that she had previously observed through the glass door on the previous evening, and she witnessed O'Shaughnessy leaving the area in her vehicle at about 8:30 a.m.

On the same date, after not observing Gutman or his vehicle in the area throughout the morning, Moneypenny ended the surveillance of this location at approximately 10 a.m. She then drove by the Eastham Court address, where she also observed no sign of Gutman. She signed off at this location at about 10:15 a.m.

On the same date, at approximately 3:15 p.m., a third investigator, Claude Lebel, arrived at the Mapleview Court address, where he did not observe either the subject's or O'Shaughnessy's vehicles. Lebel remained at the location observing the subject's home from a distance of approximately 1,500 feet until about 6:15 p.m., when he signed off. Investigator Lebel did not observe Gutman, O'Shaughnessy or either of their vehicles during this timeframe.

On June 15, 2007, at approximately 5:45 a.m., I returned to the Mapleview Court address, where I did not observe the subject's vehicle, although the Chevy was present. I conducted periodic surveillance on the location throughout the morning, until signing off at about 9 a.m. I did not observe O'Shaughnessy, Gutman or the latter's vehicle during this timeframe.

On the same date, at approximately 3:40 p.m., Investigator Lebel returned to the Mapleview Court address, where he observed that the Ford Explorer was again parked in front of the townhouse. He noted that the door was again open, and the same dog was observed through the glass of the outer door. Lebel periodically checked the area until about 3:30 p.m. and noted that the subject's vehicle remained in the same location throughout this timeframe.

On the same date, at approximately 4:30 p.m., I again arrived at the Mapleview Court address, and I observed the subject's car parked in the parking lot in front of the home. At about 4:50 p.m., I then witnessed Gutman exit the house, get in the Jeep Cherokee and leave the area. The subject was wearing a blue baseball cap, a gray shirt and shorts. After watching the home for some time and observing no other activity, I signed off at approximately 5:15 p.m.

On June 16, 2006, I returned to the Mapleview Court address at approximately 8 p.m., when I observed that the subject's vehicle was parked in front of the home. The Chevy was not present at this time. At about 11:30 p.m., I placed a single penny on the subject's rear passenger tire and ended the surveillance. I did not observe Gutman on this date.

On June 17, 2006, at approximately 6:30 p.m., I again returned to the location, where I observed both the Explorer and the Chevy. The penny that I had placed on the former vehicle's tire was no longer present, which suggests that the vehicle had been moved since June 16. After being unable to secure a spot from which to watch the home, I signed off the surveillance on this day at about 7 p.m.

Appendix C

REPORT STYLE GUIDELINES

This guidebook was based on the original one prepared by Scott Krischke for our firm. It was inspired by the style guidelines used by journalists in reporting breaking news. It has been modified over the years as the firm's style has evolved to become more applicable for investigators, as opposed to journalists. It is intended to address many of the common questions that our new investigators have about the style that we use in preparing our firm's memos. It is also intended to address the most common errors that we have encountered in the thousands of reports that we have reviewed. The guidebook opens up with a few fundamental principles for good report-writing, including specific grammatical rules and punctuation. Following this is an alphabetical list of rules for common questions arising in drafting reports. It is meant to be used as a reference during report writing to allow the writer to follow a stated, consistent policy so that all reports follow a uniform style. For instance, it sets out specific rules for how to write out ages, dates and occupational titles. Note that these guidelines are specific to reports, not running resumes, which have much less stringent style requirements. Also note that this stylebook does not cover everything that one needs to know about grammar in the English language. For a good treatise on basic grammar, syntax and punctuation, refer to *The Elements of Style*.

Style Fundamentals of Report-Writing

1. Be careful with pronouns.

If the goal of investigative documentation is to provide your clients with clear, understandable summations of your investigative endeavors, the first thing that needs to be regulated is the use of pronouns. Pronouns—

he, she, they, them and it—are fundamental to the fabric of the English language. They are used to shorten speech, to avoid repetition and even to convey familiarity. However, when used improperly, pronouns can destroy an investigative report. A good rule of thumb is to never use pronouns when you are discussing two subjects in a sentence or are in the midst of discussing multiple subjects. It is okay to refer to a witness with a pronoun if they are only speaking about themselves or no one else has been injected into the discussion. However, once that witness brings up co-workers, friends, family or even items, using pronouns becomes dangerous. Consider the following example:

> Connor said that he was employed at Belfast Pharmaceuticals since he arrived in the United Kingdom. He added that he only left Belfast because he was offered so much money elsewhere.

This is acceptable because Connor is the only one speaking, and no other subjects are being addressed. However, when a witness brings more people or things into a conversation, pronouns start to become a concern. For example:

> Connor said that he and Bill Russell worked together for three years. He said that **he** always came to work at 8 a.m., and **he** never saw anything out of the ordinary about **his** performance.

Who is coming in at 8 a.m.? Russell or Connor? Did he mean that Russell never saw anything out of the ordinary, or Connor never noticed anything out of the ordinary? Whose performance? It may seem a little unnatural, but it is always best to err on the side of caution and to use complete names when you are discussing multiple subjects. Rewritten, the above paragraph should read:

> Connor said that he and Bill Russell worked together for three years. He said that **Russell** always came to work at 8 a.m., and **Connor** never saw anything out of the ordinary about **Russell's** performance.

In this example, we know exactly to who Connor is referring, and we are left with a much more clear report of the facts of the case.

2. Quote consistently.

The key to all proper style is consistency, and the place where inconsistency is most noticeable is in quotations. Quotes are extremely important to our cases and our clients because they are a verbatim statement of what a witness told us. Adding quotes to reports is our way of letting our witnesses "speak for themselves," directly to our clients. Direct quotes commonly can make or break a case at trial. Therefore, we should be careful to always institute a consistent policy for documenting quotes. Our rule is that all quotes that are the start of a sentence begin with the first word capitalized. If they are taken from the middle of a larger quote, they should be left un-capitalized. Periods, commas and other punctuation at the end of a quote always go inside the quotation marks. A comma should always follow an introductory word to a quotation, unless it is a quote taken from a larger quote used to describe something briefly.

Example:

Wrong: When asked what she does for a living, Swardson said "what you need to do is talk to my boss. He can tell you what I do".

Correct: When asked what she does for a living, Swardson said, "What you need to do is talk to my boss. He can tell you what I do."

Notice that there is a comma following the word "said," to introduce the quotation, that the first word of the quotation is capitalized, and that the period ending the second sentence is within the quotation marks.

Example:

Correct: Dobbs said that he was "fairly certain" that the company laid off employees in the final quarter of last year.

Here, since we are using a quick statement from the middle of a larger statement that Dobbs said, we do not need capitalization or introductory commas. For quotes ending with a statement from the author, you should use a comma within the quotation.

Example:

Correct: "Every time that I showed up to his house, there were people doing drugs," Michaels said.

Notice the comma following the word "drugs" within the quotation, before finishing the sentence outside of the quotation.

Utilizing a consistent policy of documenting quotations will show your clients that you are professional and recognize the importance that quotations can play in a case.

3. Never write in the second person.

We write our reports from the position of unbiased observers—people who reiterate what others have said. The goal is to put our readers in front of the interview as it happens as much as possible. While common in ordinary conversation, casual references to a hypothetical "you" are too informal, halting, confusing and will often disrupt the flow of a report. You are writing to a client about objective facts. The reader, however, is not going to differentiate objective facts from any subjective statements that you may have inadvertently included the report; the reader only cares about clarity. Therefore, the only time that the word "you" should be written in a report is when it is in a direct quote from a witness.

Examples:

Wrong: When asked what the waiters did when they checked in, Grossman said that **you** typically enter the restaurant at 3 p.m. and clock in when you receive your first customer.

Correct: When asked what the waiters did when they checked in, Grossman said that **the waiters** typically will enter the restaurant at 3 p.m., and they will clock in when they receive their first customer.

4. Use an active voice.

Using a strong active voice in reports connotes confidence and allows for a direct, easy-to-read report for our clients. Verbs that are preceded by the words "was" or "had been" are dead ringers for a passive voice. To the reader, use of the passive voice makes the investigator appear unsure of what he or she is writing. To use the active voice, you place the subject immediately before the verb, with nothing between them. Unless absolutely necessary or in a direct quote, "passive voice" should be avoided at all costs and should replaced instead by an active voice.

Examples:

Wrong: Anderson said that **he was hit by the police officers** immediately after he was pulled out of the car.

Wrong: **It was not remembered** whether or not Thompson clocked in to work on March 7, 2010.

Wrong: Sen. McCain stated that he never knew that the report **had been delivered by his staff assistant**.

Correct: Anderson said that **the police officers pulled him out** of the car and immediately began to hit him.

Wrong: Thompson could not remember whether or not **he clocked in to work** on March 7, 2010.

Correct: Sen. McCain stated that he never knew that his staff assistant **delivered the report**.

5. Use identifications consistently.

When shortening names after their first reference in a report, even the best-writing investigators can forget how they first identified a person, place or entity in an investigative report. But these mistakes can be extremely costly to the investigator: they communicate to a client that you are disorganized or reckless with your reports and undermine the report's overall credibility. Therefore, you must pay special attention in reviewing a report to make sure that all identifiers are consistent. This also carries over to separate reports on the same case.

Examples:

Wrong: Asked where he worked while living in Virginia, Mosby said that he was an architectural professor at **Virginia Polytechnic Institute and State University ("Virginia Tech")** ... (*two pages later*) ... Mosby added that he felt that VA Tech was a great place to work and he would return back there at some point in his life.

Correct: Asked where he worked while living in Virginia, Mosby said that he was an architectural professor at **Virginia Polytechnic Institute and State University ("Virginia Tech")** ... (*two pages later*) ... Mosby added that he felt that **Virginia Tech** was a great place to work and he would return back there at some point in his life.

Style Guide

Acronyms/Abbreviations

Care should be taken to avoid unfamiliar acronyms, abbreviations or technical jargon that may confuse readers. Only very common abbreviations may be used in a report without first using the full term and then including the abbreviation in parentheses. As a general rule of thumb, any acronym that could be not be immediately identified by the average person on the street must be written out in full the first time it is mentioned in a report, with the acronym itself following it within parentheses and quotations. See Appendix A for the bolded abbreviations that do not require the author to first write out the term.

Examples:

I asked Orace whether he has spoken to anyone else about this, and he said that he spoke to an FBI agent, whose name he could not remember. Orace said that he believes the agent's name was Simon LNU.

Orace later told me that he also spoke with an investigator from the Bank of America ("BoA"). Orace said that the investigator with BoA was named Sonia Delmar.

Addresses

When written in full, addresses should be as they appear on a letter with the street address, the street name, followed by the municipality, full name of a state and zip code (if known). Abbreviations for street types ("St." for "Street," "Ave." for "Avenue") and directions of a street (e.g., "E." for "East," "W." for "West") can be abbreviated.

Example:

Stanley said that he lives at 1865 W. Fullerton Ave., Chicago, Illinois 60614.

Ages

Age should always be listed in digital numbers with hyphens used to separate the words in listed ages. If writing an age in lists, without "years-old" following it, those ages are always in digital format regardless of the age, and will be separated with commas.

Examples:

He said that he had a 3 year old daughter.
Asked for her age, she said that she is 29 years old.

He said she was with her three sons, aged 3, 6 and 9.

Aliases

Aliases will be listed in the "also known as" format, utilized by federal law enforcement and intelligence agencies, as "a/k/a" in lower-case letters. Note that this information typically forms an independent clause that must be enclosed with commas.

Example:

With reference to the above I was tasked with locating Sebastian Tombs, a/k/a Sugarman Treacle, a/k/a ST.

If an interview subject knows the individual only by his or her alias, that alias will take the place of that person's last name in the investigative reports and be written out following the word "hereafter" in parentheses, with the nickname in quotes.

Example:

Cole said that he only knew Merton as "Bubbles," (hereafter "Bubbles") and that he hung out in the neighborhood from time to time. Bubbles was an auto mechanic, Cole said.

All right

This phrase must always be written as two words, never as "alright."

Attachments

References to attachments should be included within the body of the report, either in parentheses or by otherwise naming the attached document. Only official documents, such as court records, or documents produced by the witness, such as diagrams or organizational charts, should be attached to reports. Never attach notes, investigative database printouts or other working documents to a report.

Examples:

According to a press release from the Securities and Exchange Commission (attached), the bank is presently under investigation by the FBI.

The company's 2008 K-10 Report, which is attached to this investigative report, lists nearly $108 million in liabilities.

Author

On report headers, make the author's name capitalized and include your initials after your name in parentheses, as these can be used to more easily identify you to clients in the running resume and on invoices.

Example:

FROM: THOMAS MAGNUM (TSM)

Biographical Paragraph

The first paragraph in every report should include the subject's basic biographical information, including full first and last name, and the location of the interview and the physical description of the subject (if known and applicable). The subject's Social Security number, date of birth and any additional contact information should also be included in this paragraph, provided the information is confirmed.

Example:

With reference to the above case, we interviewed Hal Kines, SSN unknown, DOB unknown, on December 20, 2010, by meeting with him at ABC Bank, located at 1711 Massachusetts Ave. NW, Washington, DC 20036.

Case Numbers

The first letters of the term "Case Numbers" should be capitalized when immediately preceding a court or other type of case number. The term should never be capitalized when used on its own. All of the letters in case numbers should be capitalized, even if the court jurisdiction where the case originated does not capitalize its case numbers.

Examples:

Trevor was charged with possession of a controlled substance in the U.S. District Court of the Northern District of Virginia (Alexandria). The case number is 1:2008CR1424.

In Prince George's County Circuit Court, Case Number 00636332E1, Kines was charged with illegally brandishing a handgun.

Cellular Phones

Cellular phone should be written as two words. It must be written out in full when distinguishing a known cellular phone number from a landline. The term mobile phone is also acceptable. Do not use "cell phone," unless part of a quote from a subject.

Examples:

Nixon provided 312-555-0069 as his cellular phone number during the interview.

"He called me on my cell phone," Ford said, referring to his contact with Carter.

Citations

Investigators must always cite where they learned the information in their reports. If this information came from a formal source, it may be cited in a footnote. Normally, however, the information came from a human source, surveillance or a database. Information obtained from a database could be accredited to "credit header information" or an "investigative database."

Examples:

According to an investigative database, Reagan has a connection to 104 Main St. in Fairfax, Virginia. However, I went to the aforementioned address and learned from a neighbor, whose name I do not know, that Reagan has not lived there in more than five years. When I later called Jane Wyman, who is believed to be Reagan's girlfriend, she told me that Reagan presently resides in Nebraska.

Commas

Our firm does not use serial commas, which are the commas that sometimes take place in a list immediately preceding the conjunction (i.e., or, and or but). However, this is a matter of policy–not grammar. Serial commas are perfectly acceptable, provided they are used consistently.

Examples:

We searched the following Virginia counties for criminal records: Fairfax, Arlington and Prince William.

One major area concerning commas in investigative reports relates to non-restrictive relative clauses. These are dependent clauses that are contained within sentences that can stand alone as complete sentences. These types of clauses must be enclosed with commas to offset them from the rest of the sentence.

Examples:

With reference to the above case, I interviewed John Adams, SSN unknown, DOB unknown, on March 24, 2011.

When asked if he had previously been aware of the theft, Jefferson said that, had I not contacted him for an interview, he would have never known anything about it.

In the above examples, "SSN unknown," "DOB unknown" and "had I not contacted him for an interview" are all non-restrictive relative clauses. Like all types of dependent clauses, they cannot stand alone as complete sentences. Notice that if you remove any of them from the sentence, what remains is still a complete sentence.

Contractions

Investigators should not use contractions in investigative reports, unless the contraction is part of a direct quote contained within quotation marks.

Examples:

He told me that he would not be calling me back unless the general counsel told him that it was okay for him to cooperate in our investigation.

She said, "Don't call me again!" and then hung up the phone.

Counties

Formal names of counties will have the first letter of each word capitalized. The word "County" is capitalized when it is directly following the name of the county, but the plural of the word, "counties," is not capitalized.

Examples:

When she got the job, she moved to Fairfax County.

Since 1990, he has lived in Lake, Cook and DuPage counties, Illinois.

Countries

Names of formal countries will have the first letter of each word capitalized. Always write out the words United States and United Kingdom, unless they are used as an adjective, in which case you should write U.S. and U.K., respectively.

Examples:

Jiminez said that her family immigrated to the United States from Costa Rica in 1995.

He said that he worked for a U.S. government agency, but he was not more specific.

Dates

Dates in reports will be listed in two ways. In the header of the report, the date's month will be written out in capital letters followed by a digital day and year number.

Example:

DATE: MAY 15, 2007

All dates listed in reports after the initial header listing will be done in the same format but without the capitalization. When only a month and year is known, do not include the word "of" between the month and year.

Examples:

I interviewed her at approximately 2 p.m. on August 8, 2008.

He said that on the day in question, February 11, 2008, he was taking a mid-term exam.

Jackson said that he graduated medical school in June 2007.

Departments

When listing the names of formal departments within companies or agencies, the first letters of the title of the department should be listed entirely in capital letters. On second reference, the word "department" can be dropped, but the first letter of the title of that department should remain capitalized. Keep in mind, a formal subsection of a business, organization or agency need not be referred to as a "department" to qualify for this; this could include divisions and teams, for example. In some cases, it may be difficult to determine if a term used by a witness is actually the title of a department or just a colloquial term used to describe the department. In these instances, the investigator should err on the side of capitalizing the term anyway.

Examples:

Medwick said that Jackson worked in the Technology Department with him.

It carried on like that for two weeks, he said, before he was finally transferred to Marketing.

DiMaggio then put in a request to move to the Security Officers Management Branch at the agency headquarters.

Disclaimer

For interview reports, include a "disclaimer" (second) paragraph to clearly indicate that you communicated the nature of the interview and that the subject knew who you were and agreed to speak to you regarding the case. The way that you identify yourself to subjects should be the same in every case, so that you can always answer reliably what you told witnesses about your identity.

Example:

After being advised of the identity of the interviewer and the nature of the investigation, Roger Clemens agreed to be interviewed regarding the matter of thefts and controls at ABC Bank and told us the following.

Effective and Affective

Effect means "result," and affect means "to influence." They are both adjectives although "affect" may also be used as a verb. Effective means bringing about a result. Affective on the other hand means to influence somebody emotionally. Since investigating often involves establishing causal relationships, the correct word is most often going to be effective.

Examples:

Asked about Ford's skills as a manager, Carter said that Ford was generally effective, yet inconsistent.

Taft was not sure whether or not the news affected Thompson's ability to work

Footers

The report's ending should be clearly delineated with a footer that lists the author's initials and names the person who reviewed the report. Note that this is not a true footer, like one that you can create in Microsoft Word, because it does not necessarily go on the bottom of the page; rather, the line on the footer is two spaces from the last paragraph in the report, meaning that it is often placed in the middle of the page. The line of the footer can easily be replicated in Microsoft Word by hitting the underscore key a few times on a fresh line and then hitting the enter key. The font in the footer should be the maximum size that allows for the information to be contained on two lines. The link to our company web site should be accessible when the document is viewed electronically.

Example:

This completes this Investigative Memo, prepared by JSB and reviewed by James Watson, both investigators for Dinolt Becnel & Wells Investigative Group LLC, online at www.dinolt.com.

Font

The text is in Times New Roman, 12-point font, save for the title "INVESTIGATIVE REPORT," which is in 16-point font. All of the text in the report's header is capitalized for emphasis.

Geography

Mention of properly-named rivers, lakes, oceans, mountains, deserts, etc. should all be done with the first letters of the geographical subject capitalized.

Examples:

He said that he had just returned from his visit to the Rocky Mountains and was not yet back in the loop with what was happening with the team.

After exiting Interstate 95, she followed several side roads until she reached Chesapeake Bay.

Government Agencies/Bodies:

Formal government agencies or bodies on any level (federal, state, local) will be capitalized. Commonly-known acronyms (i.e.: CIA, FBI, DEA) can be used on first reference, but all other agencies should only be referenced by its acronym after a designation following its full name.

Examples:

Collins, who has worked for the States Attorney of Maryland in Prince George's County for nine years, said that he did not remember Crawford.

He stated that he had previously worked for the Defense Intelligence Agency ("DIA") for 12 years before coming to work at Lockheed Martin.

He added that he has a friend who worked in the Massachusetts House of Representatives.

It was not before she came to Chicago Streets and Sanitation ("CSS") that she realized how bad he had it, she said.

Height

Physical dimensions of subjects will be listed in a combination of digits and words. You should always use numerical symbols for height. Note that it is acceptable to use an apostrophe to designate feet and a quotation mark to designate inches (e.g., 6'2") in the running resume, but this format should never be used in a report.

Example:

He is described as 6 feet 2 inches tall.

Holidays

Holidays must be capitalized and spelled out when used in reference to a day recognized to be a holiday by the federal government, a church or popular culture. This will not include individual days of importance, such as birthdays and anniversaries, which are never capitalized.

Examples:

He said that he remembered the incident occurred on Halloween, a little after midnight.

The two were home celebrating their anniversary on the night in question, she said.

He said that he was home visiting his family for Christmas.

Hyperlinks

Reports should never contain hyperlinks to outside sources, except for in the report's footer, which should contain a link to the company web site. When writing down web site addresses in the body of the report, leave off the "www." and the transfer protocol (e.g., "http://") to avoid inadvertently creating a hyperlink. Include longer Web addresses in a footnote, rather than putting them in the body of the report.

Internet

The words Internet and Web (when referring to the Internet) should always be capitalized, except for the term "web site." (See "web site").

Job Titles

Job titles should not be capitalized under any circumstances, except in the case of a military or law enforcement ranking or an elected member of the government. Do not capitalize formal titles of business leaders or citizens. Do not capitalize titles not attached to names. However, it is permissible to capitalize names of formal departments within an office that are part of a title, just not the actual title following that department.

Examples:

He said that one of his Army supervisors, Sgt. Mel Ott, told him to do that.

The incident occurred on a day when Sen. Barack Obama was speaking at the school.

Asked for his position at Ame Industries, Carew said that he was a vice president.

She said that she would one day like to run to be a member of Congress.

When asked for the name of his supervisor, Johnson said that it was Human Resources director Andrew Sullivan.

Laws

References to specific legal acts passed by federal, state or local government will be written with capital letters and, where necessary and deemed appropriate by the writer, will be abbreviated after their first mention. In very limited circumstances, when a law is either very well known by its acronym or when a violation of a law is the actual subject of the report, then it may be abbreviated in its first appearance without first spelling out the formal name of the law.

Examples:

He said that he was convicted of a felony under the Uniformed Controlled Substances Act ("UCSA").

He said that he understands the Uniformed Services Employment and Reemployment Act ("USERRA") and felt that this was a "clear violation" of it.

She said that she submitted a FOIA request for the information, but she never heard back from the agency.

References to specific laws that do not have proper names listed after the laws signed into act by an elected body will not be capitalized.

Examples:

In 1996, he was charged with burglary and possession of burglarious tools in San Bernardino County, California.

He was confined to jail during that time, due to his arrest for possession of controlled dangerous substances in 2002.

Margins

The report's margins are exactly one inch on each side. The body of the report is always justified.

Names:

1. People

All proper names must have the first letter capitalized. When a first name is not known, the writer will use the abbreviation "FNU," meaning "first name unknown." When a last name is not known, the writer will use the abbreviation "LNU," which should be in parentheses if the subject just did not say the last name and without parentheses if the subject actually indicated that he or she does not know the person's name.

Examples:

With reference to the above I was tasked with interviewing witness Grover Alexander. Upon identification and references to the case in question, Alexander agreed to be interviewed provided that he first checked with his boss, Mike (LNU). Smith returned to a phone a few minutes later and told me that his boss said it was okay for him to talk.

Alexander then told me, without being asked, that he saw Andy LNU steal the money. Asked about Andy's last name, Alexander said that he does not know it.

Presumably, in the above examples, Alexander knows what his boss's last name is-he just did not mention it to the investigator—but he told us expressly that he does not know Andy's last name.

After the first reference of that person, the writer will refer to that person only by his or her last name, except in the event that more than one reference to that last name is made for different people, in which case the writer should use all of the subject's first names after the first reference to the person's full name. This is sometimes necessary in cases involving families or where subjects have very common names. Possessives in names will be referenced as they would normally.

Example:

Bond's brother worked alongside Mathewson's best friend, Whitey Ford. Ford's shop is located somewhere in Adams Morgan in Washington, DC, Bond said.

The investigator should avoid using pronouns when using the person's last name would be clearer. A good rule of thumb is to always use a last name, not a pronoun, immediately following the mention of another person of the same gender.

Example:

I asked Frank Robinson what he saw when he looked out the window, and he said that he saw Johnny Damon hanging by his feet from Robinson's balcony. Robinson said that, after he saw Damon hanging there, Robinson was so shocked he immediately fell over backwards.

In the case of junior or senior distinction in the names of a subject, that distinction will be abbreviated and follow the name without a comma.
Example:

Dean said that his father's hero had always been John F. Kennedy Jr.

2. Businesses and Organizations

All proper names of businesses and organizations will be listed in investigative reports with the first letter of each word capitalized. At the discretion of the writer, a business may be listed as an abbreviation or an acronym, however this must be done only after the business's complete name is referenced. The exception for this is commonly known organizations or businesses, such as FBI or IBM.

Example:

After being advised of the identity of the interview and the nature of the call, Cobb agreed to be interviewed regarding his employment with the FBI and his subsequent relationship with an employee of Heckler & Koch (hereafter "H&K").

Possessives for businesses and organizations will follow the same rules as people.

Numerals

Numbers will be listed in the Associated Press style format. Numbers "0" through "9" will be written out, except in the case of ages, heights, proper names or used in forming names (as in addresses). Anything 10 or above will be listed as numeric digits.

Examples:

His supervisor said that he was late to work eight times.

His supervisor added that he called in sick at least 15 times since starting work last year.

He said that he had a 9-year-old sister.

He said that his brother lived at 2424 6th St., NW, Washington, DC.

Page Numbers

All reports must include page numbers on the lower, right-hand corner. The first page does not require a page number.

Paragraphs

There should always be a biographical paragraph, followed by a disclaimer paragraph (see disclaimer in this appendix). After the disclaimer paragraph, the paragraphs must be chronological and grouped by topic. Each new topic introduced in the chronology requires a new paragraph. All paragraphs are separated by one space and are never indented.

Example:

Kines explained that they had two hammer drills in the shop, but he dropped his and it broke, so Dalmas ordered him another one. Asked what happened to the broken one, he said that he does not know. He said that there are still two drills at ABC Property Management.

Asked if he is on the Home Depot account, Kines said that Dalmas was the only one on the Home Depot account up until this week, as he has to do the ordering now that Dalmas no longer works there.

Kines said that another drill did come into the shop, and he does not know what happened to it.

Persons

When followed by a number, the correct term is persons, not people. Otherwise, you should use the word people.

Examples:

I observed four persons enter the building at approximately 3:44 p.m. I recognized one person as Reagan.

She said that people generally respect her at work; they are only complaining about her because they are jealous.

Phone Numbers

Phone numbers will be listed in digital format, with hyphens separating long-distance area codes, prefixes and suffixes. No number "1" will be listed before these numbers, nor will they be confined to parentheses.

Example:

I called her at phone number 703-328-0905 at approximately 2 p.m. on January 29, 2008.

During the course of the interview, he provided 212-178-4350 as a contact number.

Quotes

An investigator should use quotes when appropriate to record exactly what witnesses said during interviews. However, you should take great care to ascertain that quote marks were also used in the notes taken during the interview itself. It is okay to use brackets inside of quotes to paraphrase a quote or to make it fit grammatically within a sentence, provided that the exact meaning of the quote is not altered. Also, if the statement in the quotation marks is a complete sentence, then there should be a comma before the quotation marks and the statement's first word should be capitalized. Note that other punctuation marks always go inside the final quotation mark. For more about quotation marks, refer to the Style Fundamentals of Report Writing at the beginning of Appendix C.

Examples:

Spahn said that Snyder exclaimed, "Get your hands off me!"

I asked Fox about the money, and he replied, "He [McGuire] took it."

She repeatedly expressed dissatisfaction with her job, at one point stating that she has "had it" with the company and wants to "go far, far away."

Race and Ethnicity

If racial or ethnic details of a subject are to be included in an investigative report, the adjectives "white" and "black" should always be used in the place of Caucasian or African American, unless the subject is respectively a citizen of an African county as well as an American, or from the Caucasus region of Eastern Europe. If the subject appears to be of East Asian descent (such as Chinese or Korean), that subject will be referred to as "Asian." Subjects who appear to be of Indian, Pakistani or Sri Lankan origin should be referred to as "South Asian." People from Central and South American descent should be referred to as "Hispanic." Those who appear to come from the Middle East should be referred to as "Middle Eastern." The exception to these rules is when it is made known to the investigator the specific country or region from which that person draws his or her heritage—for instance: Mexican, Chinese, Australian, Arab, etc.—in which case it is acceptable to include their country of origin. Race details should be kept as nonspecific as possible when they are unknown. For example, the investigator should not describe a subject based on a particular region of the world, such as "European" or "Central American," unless it is known firsthand that the person is of that descent.

Examples:

He is described as a white male, approximately 60-years-old, with gray hair.

Asked if her brother is also Mexican, she said that he is half Mexican and half Chilean.

Regions

When a cardinal directional region of a state, city or neighborhood is mentioned, the first letter of that region will be capitalized as well.

Examples:

She said that she had been living in Southern California for five years at that time.

The original headquarters of the office was based in South Chicago, he said.

He told police that his brother purchased the weapon in North Brooklyn.

Recipients

The main recipient of a report is the person most likely to read and act on the information in the report. It may be an associate or a legal assistant. Beyond these guidelines, however, whenever there is a question of who should be listed as the report's primary recipient, it should always go to the most senior of the two individuals. In the CC section of the template, all of the remaining recipients should be listed, including the case manager of the investigative firm. In the event that the report only had one recipient, the CC section of the report should be left blank; it should not be removed from the template.

Semicolons

Semicolons are particularly useful in investigative reports to help delineate complex items in large lists. We also use them between names in our report headers.

Examples:

CC: MICKEY COCHRANE; LEFTY GROVE; REGGIE JACKSON

According to credit header sources, he has resided in Washington, DC; Arlington, Fairfax, Prince William and Suffix counties, Virginia; and Prince George's, Montgomery and Frederick counties, Maryland.

Sources

Residency is attributed to "credit header information" when gleaned from databases. This is important, as the only way to verify residency is to actually witness the subject living at the address. Investigative databases really only show that someone has had a connection to a given address. Always include some of the information that was provided at the initiation of the investigation that leads you to conclude that the subject or subjects discussed in the interview are the correct people.

Examples:

Devlin told me that she learned from Rachel LNU that Hubell is presently residing in Mississippi. Through an investigative database search, I was able to locate a possible address for Hubell in Biloxi.

A neighbor informed me that Hubell no longer lives at this address. I then ran her name in the Bureau of Prisons ("BoP") inmate database and discovered that she is presently incarcerated in Kansas.

Spacing

Only hit the space bar one time after a period. Also, there should be only one line of spacing between paragraphs, and two lines of spacing between the final paragraph of the report and the footer.

States

States should be capitalized and written out in full in reports, even when they are listing a postal address. This is helpful in preventing confusion regarding postal codes that may not be familiar to the readers. The exception to this rule is the District of Columbia, which should be referred to simply as "Washington, DC." The reason for the exception is that the District of Columbia is actually more recognizable by its abbreviation. When citing a state in a phrase that begins with "State of . . ." or "Commonwealth of . . ." the first word of the phrase needs to be capitalized.

Examples:

I interviewed him at approximately 6 p.m. at his home, located at 112 Chestnut St., St. Louis, Missouri 10223.

She said that her daughter currently lives in Montana, but had once lived in Maryland and in the Commonwealth of Virginia.

The second interview was conducted at the law firm's Washington, DC office.

Time

Time will be written out in digital numbers, with segments of full hours listed digitally, followed by "a.m." or "p.m." to distinguish time of day. When needed for clarification purposes, use the abbreviations for Eastern, Central, Mountain and Pacific Standard Times. It is not necessary to include zeros following whole hours.

Examples:

He said that he arrived home at approximately 6 p.m.

The incident occurred around 7:45 a.m., according to Cera.

Speaker was in Las Vegas, so he did not learn of Brock's termination until 8 a.m., p.s.t.

Title

Reports should be named in a manner that will make them easier to retrieve later. The date should be listed first, followed by the month and the

day–both in a two-digit format. This is to make a list of reports for the same case chronologically when they are stored in a digital file. After the date, the investigator should name it in the most straightforward manner possible. The name should succinctly describe what is in the report.
For occupational titles, see "Job Titles."

Examples:

2008_07_12_Murdoch Ian interview

2009_01_30_Devlin, Moriarty and Legrand final report

Web Site

The words "web site" should always be written out as two separate words, uncapitalized.

Example:

Harrison said that he read about the news on a web site.

Weight

Physical weight of subjects will be listed out in digits and words.

Example:

He is described as 5 feet 8 inches tall, weighing approximately 200 pounds.

Appendix D

SAMPLE STATEMENTS

Declaration of Bella Abzug

My name is Bella Abzug. I am over eighteen (18) years of age, competent to testify, and I make this declaration having personal knowledge of the following facts:

1. I attended Tysons University Law School ("TUL") from 2003 to 2006.

2. During the Summer and Fall 2005 semesters, I enrolled in TUL's Clinic for Legal Assistance to Prisoners ("CLAP"), which offers students the opportunity to gain practical legal experience by working on cases in which the clinic represents active-duty members of the armed forces in various legal matters.

3. During my first semester as a CLAP student, Prof. Martin Van Buren ran the CLAP as its Executive Director.

4. During most of my second semester, after the first one or two classes, Prof. Maya Angelou ran the day-to-day operations of the CLAP and taught the class component of the clinic with some occasional involvement from Prof. Van Buren.

5. Prof. Angelou was an excellent teacher who cared about students actually learning through their work in the clinic. She expected her students to complete high-quality work and encouraged us to work diligently.

6. Based on my observations, Prof. Angelou took a very personal approach and an extremely active role in making sure that students and

mentor attorneys properly represented the clinic's clients. For example, at the onset of every case, Prof. Angelou would always meet with the students and break down and actually teach them all the steps and possibly contingent steps of each case to make sure that the case was handled properly and that the students actually learned how to do the work.

7. In contrast, when Prof. Van Buren supervised the students, he did not clearly break down the necessary steps in each case, such that I regularly had to seek him out to learn what to do next. This made it more difficult for me to represent clients, and it necessitated actively seeking out Prof. Van Buren's advice to learn what the next step should be in a given case.

8. I also witnessed that Prof. Angelou vastly improved the organization and operations of the clinic. Prior to her arrival, the case files were not well organized and previous students' work was not well-documented. Prof. Angelou directed students to maintain much more detailed memos than were standard under Prof. Van Buren, and she created a list of documents that needed to be included in all case files. In my opinion, the changes that she instituted made it much easier for the next student working on a case to be informed about what had previously happened on the case.

9. I observed a number of interactions between Prof. Angelou and Prof. Van Buren in the classroom when they delivered joint lectures as part of the CLAP course.

10. Based on my observations, Prof. Van Buren initially seemed friendly and warm towards Prof. Angelou. He appeared to dote on her, regularly bragging about her credentials to the clinic students.

11. Over time, however, I observed that Prof. Van Buren's behavior towards Prof. Angelou changed drastically for the worse.

12. For example, on one occasion during the latter part of the semester, while we were possibly discussing issues related to Guantanamo Bay, I witnessed Prof. Van Buren rudely and blatantly interrupting Prof. Angelou in class, cutting her off mid-sentence. Prof. Van Buren then proceeded to contradict what she had just said in front of the entire class and seemingly belittled her and talked to her in a condescending way in front of my classmates and me. This seemed partic-

ularly inappropriate to me, especially given Prof. Angelou's first-hand experience serving at Guantanamo Bay.

13. On another occasion, also later in my second semester at CLAP, I witnessed a brief but tense conversation between Prof. Angelou and Prof. Van Buren. Although I did not hear the content of this conversation, which occurred in Prof. Van Buren's office and which I overheard while waiting for Prof. Angelou outside of her office, I recognized by the sharp intonations of their voices that they were having a tense disagreement. When Prof. Angelou came out to speak with me, she did not let on at all that she had just had an argument with Prof. Van Buren.

14. Since Prof. Van Buren was not the primary instructor he did not attend CLAPs very often anyway. However, it seemed that he showed up at classes even less as the semester progressed and as his relationship with Prof. Angelou appeared to deteriorate.

15. Prof. Angelou never directly indicated to me that she was experiencing any difficulties because of Prof. Van Buren.

I solemnly declare and affirm, under penalty of perjury, that the contents of the foregoing statement are true and correct to the best of my knowledge, information and belief.

_____   _____
Date   Bella Abzug

AFFIDAVIT OF MILLARD FILLMORE

My name is Millard Fillmore. I am over eighteen (18) years of age, competent to testify, and I make this declaration having personal knowledge of the following facts:

1. I previously owned and operated a licensed mortgage broker business called Fillmore Funding Solutions ("FFS") in Illinois.

2. In approximately 2009, Franklin Pierce and I, operating as FFS, decided to purchase properties in the Chicago, Illinois area that were pre-foreclosure or in early foreclosure status.

3. We located suitable properties and either Pierce or I, on behalf of FFS, purchased them with cash.

4. We then made repairs to the properties and looked to sell them.

5. James Polk, a former loan officer for Polk Mortgage who was known to me and Pierce, located home owners and/or investors to purchase the properties.

6. I understood that Polk usually located buyers at seminars and church functions.

7. Polk told me that he had located buyers through a person named Mr. Booth, whose first name I did not know at the time.

8. Polk told me that Booth was a preacher, and it was my understanding that he and Polk knew each other through a church group or organization.

9. I never met or talked to Booth.

10. Polk told me that Booth had multiple buyers lined up for our properties.

11. Polk gave me the information to run credit reports for several different people who were all prospective buyers who Booth lined up.

12. The credit reports came from Virginia, Washington, D.C., Illinois, and Mississippi, among other states.

13. In or around early 2010, I learned that Emily Carr and James Garfield were among the prospective buyers Polk and Booth located.

14. Carr and McKinney eventually purchased four properties that Pierce or I had purchased.

15. I spoke by telephone to Carr approximately three or four times during the course of the four purchases.

16. During these telephone conversations, we discussed various matters related to the purchases.

17. I initiated the calls, mostly out of courtesy and as a good business practice, using the phone number provided by Carr on her loan applications.

18. I identified myself to Carr by name, and I assumed that she recognized me as the owner of some of the properties she was purchasing. I do not recall ever specifically telling her that I was the owner of the properties.

19. I later learned that Booth had received money from Carr and Garfield and other "investors" and told them that they could purchase homes without putting up any money for the down payments other than what they had "invested" with Booth.

20. Carr, specifically, told me that Booth told her that she did not need to put up any money for the down payments on the homes she was to purchase beyond what she had already "invested" with Booth.

21. After I learned that Carr expected the down payments to come from the money she and others had already paid to Booth, I made the down payments on one or two of the purchases to ensure that the deals would close. I did this because I know from experience that houses left unattended in Chicago are ripe for immediate theft and damage.

22. I never told Carr that I made the down payments on these one or two purchases.

I solemnly declare and affirm, under penalty of perjury under the laws of the United Sates, that the contents of the foregoing paper are true and correct to the best of my knowledge, information, and belief.

_____   _____
Date   Millard Fillmore

City/County of _____
Commonwealth of Virginia

Subscribed and sworn to before me
this _____ day of _____, _____
by _____

_____Notary Public
Philip A. Becnel IV

My commission expires _____

[Insert Statement Template Here]

[Insert Sample Statement Here]

WITNESS STATEMENT

DEFENDANT:_____

ATTORNEY: _____

CASE No. _____

THIS STATEMENT IS TAKEN FROM _____

DOB:_____SOCIAL SECURITY No._____

ADDRESS:_____

TELEPHONE: (   )_____GIVEN TO:_____, INVESTIGATOR FOR

ATTORNEY _____. THIS STATEMENT WAS TAKEN AT _____

_____THIS TIME_____AND DATE_____

_____

_____

_____

_____

_____

_____

Continuation

Continuation_____

_____

_____

_____

_____

_____

_____

_____

_____

_____

_____

_____

_____

_____

_____

_____

_____

_____

_____

_____

I HAVE READ THIS _____ ( ) PAGE STATEMENT, AND HAVE HAD IT READ TO ME. I HAVE HAD ALL THE OPPORTUNITIES I DESIRE TO ADD, DELETE, AND OR CHANGE ANYTHING IN THIS STATEMENT. THIS STATEMENT IS TRUE, CORRECT, AND COMPLETE TO THE BEST OF MY KNOWLEDGE.

_____   _____
         (SIGNATURE)   (WITNESS)

SAMPLE STATEMENT

This is the statement of Casper Gutman, date of birth 12/25/1937, Social Security number unknown, address 3500 Mapleview Court, Odenton, Maryland 21113, given to Jane Moneypenny, an investigator working for attorney Perry Mason. Mr. Mason represents ABC Bank in ABC Bank vs. Circuit World Appliances, et al in US District Court for the District of Columbia. This statement was taken at

Casper Gutman   Jane Moneypenny

3500 Mapleview Court on 6/25/2006 at approximately 11:24 am.

It all started in ~~May~~ April CG when Sally, my supervisor gave me her hotmail password to download something. I did what she told me & then I kept the password because I kept the password. Later, I got fired for this shit. I was angry, you know. ~~HA~~ CG, ~~HA~~ CG, So I thought that maybe she used the same password

[margin: Jane Moneypenny]
[margin: Cooper Cotman]

for her work account. Sally and Bill kept calling me, you know. They kept calling me and asking me for the laptop back. ~~I never called them back.~~ *(w I called them back one time but then hung up. GG)* But then I went into her emails and I saw that she was talking to some attorney about hiring a private investigator to see if I was going to destroy the laptop or sell to one of our competitors or something. Then, a few days

Casper Coleman Jane Lovejoy-Jeremy

later, I see this guy sitting in his car watching my house, and I figures, that's the investigator. So when I pull out, sure enough, he starts following me. I made a sharp turn on Strawberry Lake Way and then I got behind him. He was real slick. He got out of his car like he was talking to somebody, but I took off, and then he didn't follow me no more. That's

Sample Statement

When I took the laptop to Robert at Circuit World appliances and asked him how much the information on it was worth to him. A week later, he gave me an envelope with $~~10,000~~ $9,980 CG in cash, and here we are. I never would have stole that information if Sally would have treated me right. I have read and have had read to me this 6 page statement. I have had an

Casper Cotman   Jane Loneypenny

opportunity to make any corrections, deletions, and/or additions to this statement. I solemnly affirm under penalty of perjury that this statement is true, correct and complete.

SAMPLE STATEMENT

This is the statement of Casper Gutman, date of birth 12/25/1937, Social Security number unknown, address 3500 Mapleview Court, Odenton, Maryland 2113, given to Jane Moneypenny, an investigator working for attorney Perry Mason. Mr. Mason represents ABC Bank in ABC Bank vs. Circuit World Appliances, et al. in US District Court for the District of Columbia. This stateent was taken at 3500 Mapleview Court on 6/25/2006 at approximately 11:24 a.m. _____

It all started in April when Sally, my supervisor gave me her Hotmail password to download something. I did what she told me and then I kept the password, because I kept the password later; I got fired for this shit. I was angry, you know. So I thought that maybe she used the same password for her work account. Sally and Bill kept calling me, you know. They kept calling me and asking me for the laptop back. I called them back one time but then hung up. But then I went into her emails and I saw that she was talking to some attorney about having a private investigator to see if I was going to destroy the laptop or sell to one of our competitors or something. Then, a few days later, I see this guy sitting in his car watching my house, and I figure that's the investigator. So when I pull out, sure enough, he starts following me. I made a sharp turn on Strawberry Cake Way and the I got behind him. He was real slick. He got out of his car like he was talking to somebody, but I took off and then he didn't follow me no more. That's when I took the laptop to Robert at Circuit World appliances and asked him how much the information on it was worth to him. A week later he gave me an envelope with $9,980 in cash, and here we are.

I have read and have had read to me this 6-page statement. I have had an opportunity to make any corrections, deletions, and/or additions to this statement I solemnly affirm under penalty of perjury that this statement is true, correct and complete.

INDEX

A

abbreviation
  creating a system, 24-25
  prohibitions, 24
acronyms, 43-44
  (*see also* Appendix A)
affidavits
  generally, 51-52
  drafting, 56-57
  examples, 56-57
  locations to take, 57-58
  need for affidavit, 6
  signatures, 59-60
attempted interviews
  documenting, 30-32
audio recording, 9
  need to document, 14
  pros/cons, 10

C

confidentiality
  generally, 15-16
  breach, 18
  failure of, 17
  headings, 18
  maintenance of, 18
  in oral communication, 19
  scope, 17
  where it does/does not exist, 16

D

declarations
  (*see* statements)
discovery
  confidentiality (*see* confidentiality)
  Jencks/reverse *Jencks*, 11-12
  myths, 11
document retention
  automatic delivery, 64
  criminal defense, 71
  disposal of files, 69-70
  immediate delivery, 66-67
  inactive case files, 69
  notifying clients
    of file disposal, 69-70
    of policy, 68
  organizing a filing system, 67
  policy, generally, 7-8, 63
  secure disposal, 70
  third party records, 66

E

e-mail
  as insecure documentation, 12-13
  general rules, 13-14
  maintenance of confidentiality, 18-19

J

Jencks discovery
  (*see* discovery)

N

notes
  common mistakes, 8
  correcting mistakes, 25-26
  importance of punctuation in, 11
  most important details, 23
  necessary tools, 21-22
  observation, 22
  take notes, 4

P

Principles of Investigative Documentation
  document all efforts, 4
  document retention, 7
  prepare reports, 5
  take notes, 4
  verbatim statements, 6
privilege
  (*see* confidentiality)
punctuation
  importance of, 10-11

R

reports
  generally, 35
  acronyms, 43-44
  biographical information, 39-41
  colloquial names, 44-45
  confidentiality (see confidentiality)
  "disclaimers," 41-42
  naming reports, 37
  opinions, 45-46
  post-interview research, 47
  recipients, 37-39
  review/edits, 49-50
  sourcing, 46-47
  uniform template/style, 35-36
running resume
  generally, 3-5, 10, 21, 27-28
  abbreviations prohibited, 24
  biographical data, 35
  defined, 27
  documenting attempts, 32
  documenting failures, 29
  entry examples, 28, 30, 31, 32-33
  miscellaneous data, 32
  relevance, 29
  research exceptions, 29-30
  sending to clients, 34
  updates, 30

S

statements
  generally, 51-52
  changes, 54
  examples, 53
  from hostile witnesses, 6, 52
  signatures, 59-60
surveillance documentation
  necessity, 14
  notes, 22
  adding to running resume, 32-33

T

TrackOps, 9, 27, 34, 50

U

undercover documentation
  notes during, 22

V

video recordings, 9
  need to document, 14